中国

2014

China
2014

FOREIGN LANGUAGES PRESS

First Edition 2014

ISBN 978-7-119-08945-4

© Foreign Languages Press Co. Ltd, Beijing, China, 2014
Published by
Foreign Languages Press Co. Ltd
24 Baiwanzhuang Road, Beijing 100037, China
http://www.flp.com.cn
E-mail: flp@cipg.org.cn

Distributed by
China International Book Trading Corporation
35 Chegongzhuang Xilu, Beijing 100044, China
P.O. Box 399, Beijing, China

Printed in the People's Republic of China

Foreword

The year 2014 marks the 65th anniversary of the People's Republic of China. After six and half decades, all things are now flourishing on this vast land.

Ancient China created one of the greatest human civilizations. The Great Wall, the Terracotta Army, the Forbidden City and many other achievements are known to the whole world as the best representatives of Chinese civilization. But that was yesterday. Today's China is making new achievements. Steadfastly following the path of socialism with Chinese characteristics, the Chinese people have achieved economic, political and cultural prosperity through over 30 years of reform and opening up. More importantly, China is exploring a new model for the long-expected harmonious development of its people and Nature.

This book, titled *China*, gives to the reader a comprehensive look at the yesterday, today and tomorrow of this huge and important country.

At present, China is performing an even greater miracle while experiencing tremendous transformations. It has obtained widely recognized achievements in economy, politics and society. As the world's second-biggest economy, China is the new engine driving the global economic recovery. Its prosperity is also bringing benefits to the world as a whole. Today's China, with a new target of completing the building of a moderately prosperous society in all respects, is striving to write a new chapter of its history and fulfill the Chinese Dream of the great rejuvenation of the Chinese nation.

What is happening and what is going to happen in China are what this book is all about. Previous editions have won it a good reputation among readers worldwide, as it continues to embody new contents. Serving as an encyclopedia, the book offers wider, deeper and more updated knowledge of China in a straightforward narrative style, an abundance of maps, charts, pictures and data, and colorful online content in various language versions.

We hope you will learn about, feel and understand China through this book!

Contents

001 ▶▶ Fast Facts

004 ▶▶ Land and Resources

- 006 Sea and Land Territory
- 008 Topography
- 010 Water Resources
- 012 Climate
- 013 Land
- 016 Plants and Animals
- 018 Mineral Resources

020 ▶▶ History

- 022 Ancient Civilization
- 022 Unification and Dissemination of Civilization
- 024 Post-17th-century Changes
- 026 The Path of Chinese History

038 ▶▶ Administrative Divisions

- 040 Administrative Divisions
- 042 Brief Descriptions of Provinces and Provincial-level Municipalities and Autonomous Regions
- 052 The Road to New-type Urbanization

054 ▶▶ Population and Ethnicity

- 056 Population
- 060 Ethnic Groups
- 063 Spoken and Written Languages
- 064 Religion

066 ▶▶ Political Systems and State Structure

- 068 The Constitution
- 069 Socialist System of Laws with Chinese Characteristics
- 070 Political Systems
- 074 National People's Congress
- 076 Presidency
- 076 State Council
- 077 Central Military Commission
- 078 Local People's Congresses and Local People's Governments
- 078 People's Courts
- 079 People's Procuratorates
- 079 Chinese People's Political Consultative Conference
- 080 Political Parties and Other Organizations

084 ▶▶ Foreign Relations

- 086 Foreign Policy
- 087 Friendship with Neighboring Countries
- 088 Cooperation with Other Developing Countries
- 090 Cooperation with Major Countries
- 093 Multilateral Diplomacy

098 ▶▶ Economy

- 100 Economic Development and Transformation
- 102 Economic Structural Reform
- 103 Economic Restructuring
- 105 Innovation-driven Development
- 106 All-round Opening Up
- 110 Coordinated Development of All Regions
- 112 Agriculture
- 117 Industry
- 122 Service Industry

134 ▶▶ Environmental Protection

- 136 Laws and Systems for Environmental Protection
- 137 Coping with Climate Change
- 140 Air Pollution Control
- 142 Water Pollution Control
- 143 Forest Protection
- 144 Wetland Protection
- 145 Marine Protection
- 145 Nature Reserves
- 148 Protecting Endangered Animals and Plants
- 150 ENGOs
- 152 International Cooperation

154 ▶▶ Education and Science

- 156 Education System
- 160 Education Planning
- 162 International Exchanges
- 163 Science and Technology
- 164 Innovations in Science and Technology
- 167 International Cooperation
- 168 Social Sciences

170 ▶▶ **People's Well-being**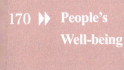

172 Income and Consumption
176 Employment
178 Social Security
179 Medical Care and Health

182 ▶▶ **Culture and Arts**

184 Libraries
186 Museums
187 Preservation of Cultural Relics
189 Intangible Cultural Heritage
191 Natural and Cultural Heritage
194 Literature
195 Opera
196 *Quyi*
197 Music
198 Dance
198 Calligraphy and Painting
200 Cinema
200 Mass Media

206 ▶▶ **Modern Life**

208 Fad
210 Sports and Fitness
212 Pastimes
214 Travel
218 Family Life
219 Traditional Festivals

222 ▶▶ **65 Years of the People's Republic**

236 ▶▶ **Appendix**

中　国　C h i n a

Located in the east of the Asian Continent and west coast of the Pacific, the People's Republic of China is the third-largest country of the world with 9.6 million sq km of land area, behind Russia and Canada.

Fast Facts

CHINA

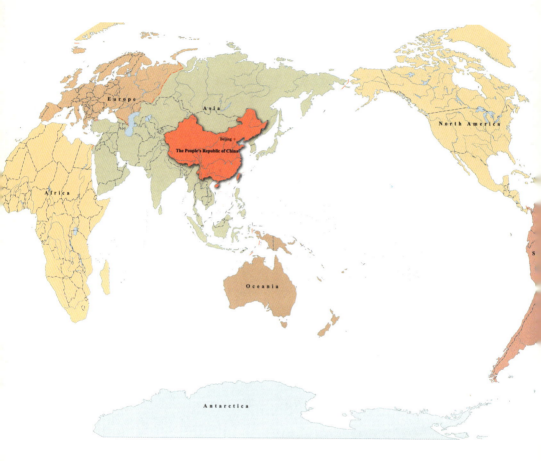

Name of the country: People's Republic of China

Capital: Beijing

Location: East Asia, to the west of the Pacific Ocean

National Flag: Five-starred Red Flag

National Emblem: Tiananmen Rostrum under the Five Stars

National Anthem: "March of the Volunteers"

National Day: October 1

National Memorial Day: December 13, for the victims of the Nanjing Massacre of 1937

Official language: Chinese

Number of ethnic groups: 56

Currency: Renminbi (RMB) / yuan

Weights and measures: metric system

Time zone: Beijing Time (UTC+8)

National Flag, Emblem and Anthem

National Flag of the People's Republic of China

National Emblem of the People's Republic of China

"March of the Volunteers"

Lyrics by: Tian Han   Music by: Nie Er

Arise, all of you who refuse to be slaves –
With our very flesh and blood, let us build
Our new Great Wall! People of China:
In this most vital hour,
Everyone must roar defiance!
Arise! Arise! Arise!
Millions of hearts with one resolve:
Brave the enemy's gunfire! March on!
Brave the enemy's gunfire! March on!
March on! March on, March on!

National Anthem of the People's Republic of China

中 国 China

Seen from above, the Chinese continent is shaped like four broad steps descending from the Qinghai-Tibet Plateau over 4,000 m above sea level on average in the west to the continental shelf zone less than 200 m deep in the east. The land area of China almost equals that of the whole of Europe. But the landform differs greatly from one place to another, as do resources.

Land
and Resources

- Sea and Land Territory
- Topography
- Water Resources
- Climate
- Land
- Plants and Animals
- Mineral Resources

Sea and Land Territory

Total land area: 9.6 million sq km

Total maritime area: 4.73 million sq km

Distance from north to south: 5,500 km

Distance from east to west: 5,200 km

Total length of land boundary: 22,800 km

Total length of coastline: 32,000 km

Adjacent seas: Bohai Sea, Yellow Sea, East China Sea, South China Sea

Bordering countries: Democratic People's Republic of Korea to the east; Mongolia to the north; Russia to the northeast; Kazakhstan, Kyrgyzstan and Tajikistan to the northwest; Afghanistan, Pakistan, India, Nepal and Bhutan to the west and southwest; and Myanmar, Laos and Vietnam to the south

Maritime neighbors: Republic of Korea, Japan, the Philippines, Brunei, Malaysia and Indonesia

A string of seven islets making up part of China's Xisha Islands

China's mainland coastline measures approximately 18,000 km, with a flat topography and many excellent harbors, most of which are ice-free all year round. The Chinese mainland is flanked to the east and south by the Bohai, Yellow, East China and South China seas, with a total maritime area of 4.73 million sq km. The Bohai Sea is China's continental sea, while the Yellow, East China and South China seas are marginal seas of the Pacific.

A total of 7,600 islands and islets dot China's territorial waters. The largest of these, with an area of about 36,000 sq km, is Taiwan, followed by Hainan, with an area of 34,000 sq km. The Diaoyu and Chiwei islands, located to the northeast of Taiwan Island, are China's easternmost islands. The many islands, islets, reefs and shoals in the South China Sea, known collectively as the South China Sea Islands, are China's southernmost island group. They are called the Dongsha, Xisha, Zhongsha or Nansha (east, west, central or south) Islands, according to their geographical locations. In 2012 the Chinese government established Sansha City. Sansha is China's southernmost city.

Diaoyu Islands

Located in the East China Sea, the Diaoyu Islands are about 356 km from Wenzhou, in east China's Zhejiang Province, 385 km from Fuzhou, capital of southeast China's Fujian Province and about 190 km from Jilong (Keelung), Taiwan Province. The Diaoyu Islands have a landmass of 4.3838 sq km, with a surrounding sea area of approximately 170,000 sq km, known as "jade in the deep sea."

Many Ming Dynasty documents, including *Voyage with a Tail Wind* (*Shun Feng Xiang Song*) published in 1403 (the first year of the reign of Emperor Yongle), *Records of the Imperial Title-conferring Envoys to Ryukyu* (*Shi Liu Qiu Lu*) written in 1532 (the 11th year of the reign of Emperor Jiajing) and *An Illustrated Compendium on Maritime Security* (*Chou Hai Tu Bian*) compiled by Zheng Ruozeng and others, all clearly demonstrate that the Diaoyu Islands belong to China.

Topography

Basins

Four major basins:

Tarim Basin in Xinjiang Uygur Autonomous Region is the largest in China.

Junggar Basin is located in the same region.

Qaidam Basin in Qinghai Province is the highest basin in China.

Sichuan Basin in Sichuan Province is the wettest.

Mountains

China has nine mountain ranges with an average elevation of 6,000 m and above, and over 20 ranges with an average altitude of 4,000 m and above. The Himalayas, the highest mountain range, extending over the border of China with India, Nepal and other countries, contain over 30 peaks of 7,300 m or higher and 11 peaks of 8,000 m or higher in elevation. Soaring 8,844.43 m above sea level is Mount Qomolangma, the world's highest peak and the main peak of the Himalayas.

Plateaus

Four major plateaus:

Qinghai-Tibet Plateau, the world's highest plateau, is considered the "roof of the world."

Inner Mongolian Plateau, in the Inner Mongolia Autonomous Region, is flanked by grasslands in the east and desert in the west.

Loess Plateau comprises all or parts of six provinces and autonomous regions, including Shaanxi and Shanxi, and is the largest of its kind in the world.

Yunnan-Guizhou Plateau, covering eastern Yunnan Province and most of Guizhou Province, has typical karst topography.

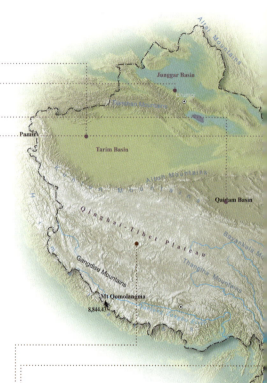

Sunset glow on Mount Qomolangma

Plains

Three largest plains:

Northeast China Plain, covering 350,000 sq km, is China's largest plain.

North China Plain is of some 300,000 sq km in central China.

Middle-Lower Yangtze Plain is of around 200,000 sq km and with a low flat terrain formed by alluvia from the Yangtze River.

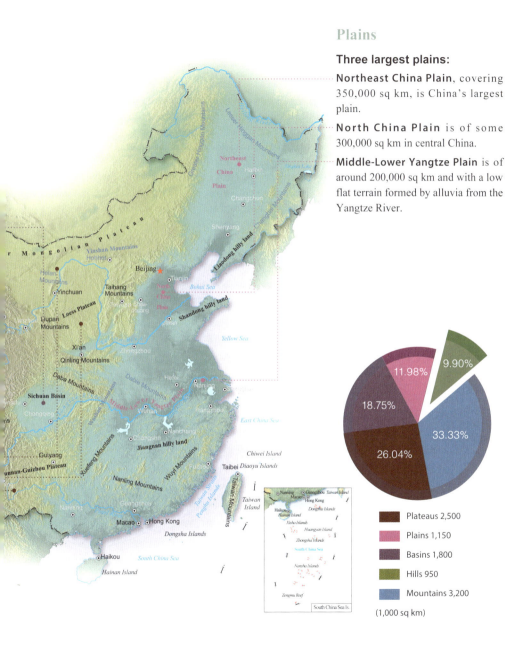

Plateaus 2,500
Plains 1,150
Basins 1,800
Hills 950
Mountains 3,200

(1,000 sq km)

Water Resources

Beijing-Hangzhou Grand Canal

In addition to rivers bestowed by nature, China has a famous manmade waterway – the Grand Canal, running from Beijing in the north to Zhejiang Province's Hangzhou in the south. Work began on the Grand Canal as early as in the fifth century BC. It links five major rivers: the Haihe, Yellow, Huaihe, Yangtze and Qiantang. With a total length of 1,801 km, the Grand Canal is the longest as well as the oldest artificial waterway in the world.

Rivers

China abounds in rivers. More than 1,500 rivers each drain 1,000 sq km or larger areas. As a result, China is rich in waterpower resources and its total hydropower reserves amount to about 680 million kilowatts, ranking first worldwide. Given its large population, China's per-capita volume of water resources is only one quarter of the world's average.

The Yangtze, 6,300 km long, is the longest river in China and the third-longest in the world. The Yangtze is a transportation artery linking west and east, its navigation benefiting from excellent natural channels.

The Yellow River is the second-longest river in China, with a length of 5,464 km. The Yellow River valley is one of the birthplaces of ancient Chinese civilization.

The Heilong River is a major river in northeast China, with a total length of 4,350 km, of which 3,101 km is in Chinese territory.

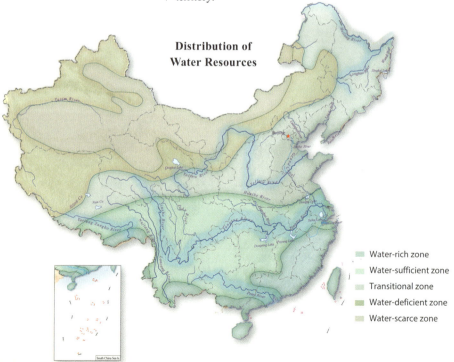

Distribution of Water Resources

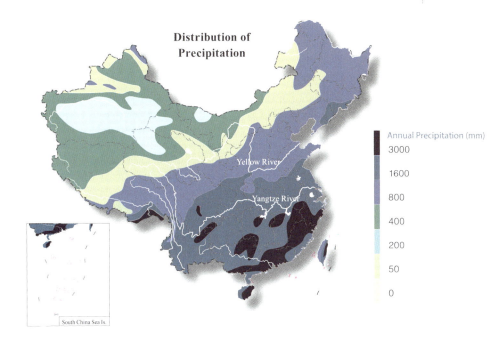

The Pearl River, 2,214 km long, is a major river in south China.
Located in southern Xinjiang, the Tarim River's 2,179 km makes it China's longest interior river.

Lakes

Most of China's lakes are found on the Middle-Lower Yangtze Plain and the Qinghai-Tibet Plateau. Freshwater lakes such as Poyang, Dongting, Taihu and Hongze mostly lie in the former area, with Poyang Lake in northern Jiangxi Province being China's largest freshwater lake; while in the latter are found saltwater lakes such as Qinghai, Nam Co and Serling Co, with northeast Qinghai Province's Qinghai Lake as the largest of its kind. Because of climate changes, however, some lakes are shrinking.

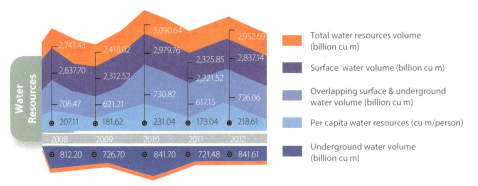

Climate

China's Five Climate Types

- Temperate monsoon climate
- Temperate continental climate
- Tropical monsoon climate
- Subtropical monsoon climate
- Plateau & Alpine climate

Most of China lies in the northern temperate zone, characterized by distinctive seasons and a continental monsoon climate. From September to April of the following year dry and cold monsoons blow from Siberia and the Mongolian Plateau, resulting in cold and dry winters, and great differences between the temperatures of north and south China. From April to September warm and humid monsoons blow from the seas to the east and south, resulting in overall high temperatures and abundant rainfall, and little temperature difference between north and south China.

In terms of temperature, the country can be sectored from south to north into equatorial, tropical, subtropical, warm-temperate, temperate, and cold-temperate zones. Precipitation gradually declines from the southeast coast to the northwest inlands, with the average annual precipitation varying greatly from place to place. In the southeastern coastal areas it is over 1,500 mm; while in northwestern areas it drops to below 200 mm.

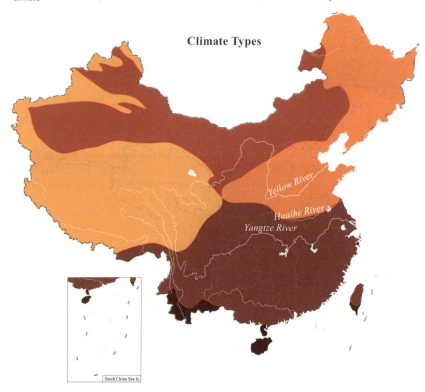

Climate Types

Danxia landscape in Qilian Mountains, Qinghai Province

Land

Cultivated land, forests, grasslands, deserts and tidelands are distributed widely across China. Cultivated land is mainly located in east China; grasslands are mainly located in the north and west; and forests mainly in the remote northeast and southwest. In China today about 1.2172 million sq km of land is cultivated; grasslands cover nearly 4 million sq km, or 41.7 percent of China's total land size; and forests cover about 2.08 million sq km, with the forest coverage rate at 21.63 percent. China's cultivated lands, forests and grasslands are among the world's largest in terms of sheer area. But due to China's large population, the per-capita areas of cultivated land, forest and grassland are small, especially in the case of cultivated land, which is less than one-third of the world's average.

North China has more cultivated land than south China, while south China has much more water than north China. For instance, on the North China Plain, which abounds in wheat and corn, cultivated land takes up about 40 percent of the national total while water resources only account for 6 percent of the national total. The imbalance of water and cultivated land worsens the water deficiency in north China, and hinders agricultural development.

Agricultural Areas

China's agricultural areas are mainly located on the Northeast China Plain, North China Plain, Middle-Lower Yangtze Plain, Pearl River Delta and Sichuan Basin. The Northeast China Plain abounds in wheat, corn, soybean, sorghum, flax and sugar beet. The North China Plain is planted with wheat, corn, millet and cotton. The Middle-Lower Yangtze Plain's low, flat terrain and many lakes and rivers make it largest production region for paddy rice and freshwater fish, hence its designation as a "land of fish and rice." This area also produces large quantities of tea and silkworms. The Sichuan Basin is green with crops in all four seasons, including paddy rice, rapeseed and sugarcane, making it known as a "land of plenty." The Pearl River Delta abounds in paddy rice, with two or three harvests a year.

Colorful fields

Terrestrial Agricultural Divisions

Forests and Pasturelands

Distribution of Forests and Pasturelands

Natural Forests

The Greater Hinggan, Lesser Hinggan and Changbai mountain ranges in the northeast are China's largest natural forest areas. Conifers and broad-leaved trees are found all over. Major tree species in the southwest include dragon spruce, fir and Yunnan pine. Often called a "kingdom of plants," Xishuangbanna in south Yunnan Province is a rare tropical broad-leaved forest area in China, playing host to more than 5,000 plant species.

Natural Pasturelands

Grasslands in China stretch several thousand kilometers from the northeast to the southwest, including quite a few centers of animal husbandry. The Inner Mongolia Prairie is China's largest natural pastureland, and home to the famed Sanhe horses, Sanhe cattle and Mongolian sheep. The natural pasturelands north and south of the Tianshan Mountains in Xinjiang are ideal for stockbreeding. The world-renowned Ili horses and Xinjiang fine-wool sheep are raised there.

CHINA

Plants and Animals

China is one of the countries with the greatest diversity of wildlife. There are 6,481 species of vertebrates, 10 percent of the world's total. Among them, 2,404 are terrestrial and 3,862 marine. China boasts more than 32,000 species of higher plants, among which are more than 7,000 species of woody plants (including 2,800 tree species), over 2,000 species of edible plants, and 3,000 species of medicinal plants. Almost all the major plants that grow in the northern hemisphere's frigid, temperate and tropical zones are to be found in China.

1	2	3
4		

1 Wild Siberian tiger
2 Golden monkeys
3 Giant panda
4 Tibetan antelopes in the wild of Hoh Xil

South China Sea Is.

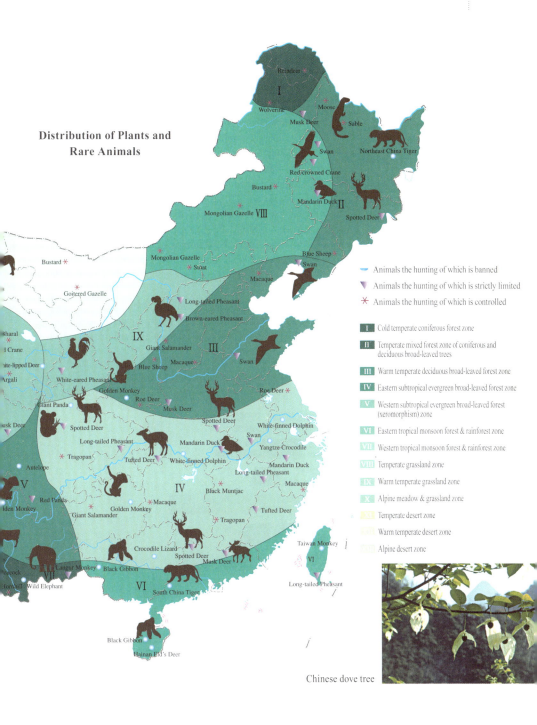

Mineral Resources

China is rich in mineral resources, and all the world's known minerals can be found here. To date, geologists have found 172 kinds of minerals in China and confirmed reserves of 159 kinds. Proven reserves of over 20 minerals are front-ranking in the world, among which the deposits of tungsten, tin, stibium, magnesite, graphite and barite are the biggest in the world. China's basic coal reserves total 279.39 billion tons, mainly distributed in northwest and north China, with Shanxi, Inner Mongolia, Shaanxi and Xinjiang leading the field. China's 22.232 billion tons of basic iron ore reserves are mainly distributed in the northeast, north and southwest. China's rare earth reserves account for about 23 percent of the world's total.

The country also abounds in petroleum, natural gas and oil shale. Petroleum reserves are mainly found in northwest, northeast and north China, as well as in the continental shelves of east China.

Output of Major Mineral Products

Increase & Decrease

Indicator	2012	2013	Change
Primary energy (billion tons of standard coal)	3.33	3.40	2.4%
Raw coal (billion tons)	3.65	3.68	0.8%
Crude oil (million tons)	207	209	1.8%
Natural gas (billion cu m)	107.22	117.05	9.4%
Crude steel (million tons)	720	780	7.6%
Gold (tons)	403.0	428.2	6.2%
Ten types of nonferrous metals (million tons)	36.722	40.549	9.7%
Phosphorus rock (million tons)	95.296	108.510	13.5%
Crude salt (million tons)	62.158	64.603	2.5%
Cement (billion tons)	2.21	2.42	9.3%

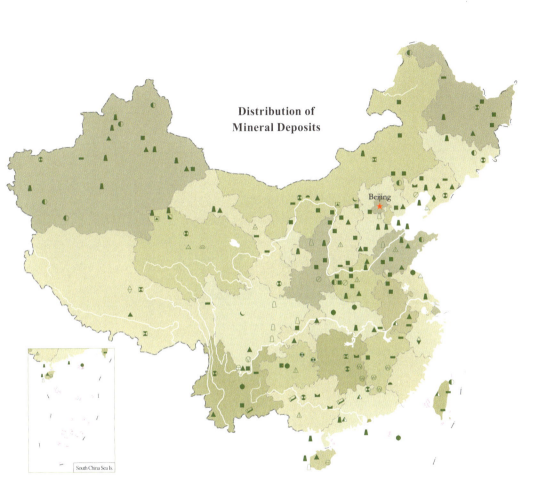

Distribution of Mineral Deposits

Metallic Minerals
- ▲ iron
- lead
- vanadium
- molybdenum
- manganese
- tin
- copper
- aluminum
- nickel
- gold
- silver
- antimony
- tungsten
- chromium
- rare earths
- mercury
- magnesium
- uranium
- lithium
- titanium

Nonmetallic Minerals
- ♦ magnesite
- underground salt
- ■ coal
- sylvine
- phosphate rock
- petroleum
- fluorite
- sulfur
- natural gas
- mica
- asbestos
- boron
- diamonds

中　国　C　h　i　n　a

The Chinese people have created a splendid civilization during a long process of historical evolution, from Da Yu's control of the floods to the "four great inventions," and from the legend of Chang'e flying to the moon to the successful flight of China's first manned spacecraft. While the ancient civilizations of Babylon, Egypt and India fell to invasion or other disasters, Chinese civilization never paused and has developed and continued to this day.

History

- Ancient Civilization
- Unification and Dissemination of Civilization
- Post-17th-century Changes
- The Path of Chinese History

Ancient Civilization

China, one of the world's most ancient civilizations, has a recorded history of nearly 4,000 years. Cultivated rice and millet as well as farming tools have been found in the Hemudu remains in Yuyao, Zhejiang Province, and the Banpo remains near Xi'an in Shaanxi Province. These relics date back 6,000 to 7,000 years. The Chinese mastered the technology of smelting bronze 5,000 years ago.

China's earliest dynasty appeared over 4,000 years ago – the Xia Dynasty (2070 BC-1600 BC). During the Shang Dynasty (1600 BC-1046 BC) iron tools came into use. Zhou Dynasty (1046 BC-256 BC) witnessed the emergence of steel production technology. During the Spring and Autumn and the Warring States periods (770 BC-221 BC), there was a great upsurge of intellectual activity, producing many famous philosophers such as Lao Zi, Confucius (Kong Zi), Mencius (Meng Zi), Mo Zi and Han Fei Zi, as well as the well-known military strategist Sun Wu, author of *Art of War*.

Jade deer of the Shang Dynasty

Owl-shaped bronze wine vessel of the Shang Dynasty

Houmuwu bronze sacrificial vessel excavated from the ruins of Yin, one of the earliest capitals of China

Bronze palace lamp of the Han Dynasty

Unification and Dissemination of Civilization

In 221 BC Qin Shi Huang (259 BC-210 BC), the First Emperor of Qin, put an end to the several hundred years of rivalry among independent principalities and established the first centralized, unified, multi-ethnic feudal state in Chinese history – the Qin Dynasty (221 BC-206 BC). From then until 1911 China was ruled by altogether 13 unified feudal dynasties and two rela-

Terracotta warriors in Mausoleum of the First Emperor of the Qin Dynasty, Shaanxi Province

tively stable multi-dynasty periods.

During these long years, the "four great inventions" – the compass, papermaking, printing and gunpowder – emerged one after another. Agriculture, handicrafts and commerce flourished, and textile, dyeing, ceramic and smelting technologies were well developed. Around the first year AD, the Han Dynasty (206 BC-AD 220) pioneered the route known as the "Silk Road," from Chang'an (today's Xi'an, Shaanxi Province) through today's Xinjiang and Central Asia, and on to the eastern shores of the Mediterranean. All types of Chinese goods, including silks and porcelains, were traded along the Silk Road. Thereafter, the "four great inventions" and other Chinese advances in science and culture successively spread all over the world.

The Tang Dynasty (618-907) pushed the prosperity of China's feudal society to its peak. By the 660s China's influence had firmly taken root in the Tarim and Junggar basins, and the Ili River valley in the far west, even extended as far as the city-states of Central Asia. During this period, extensive economic and cultural relations were established with many countries, including Japan, Korea, India, Persia and Arabia.

Amid a boom in the shipbuilding industry during the Ming Dynasty (1368-1644), Zheng He led a fleet of large ships on seven far-ranging voyages. Visiting some 30 countries, including ones in Southeast Asia and the Maldive Islands, Zheng He's fleet traversed the Indian Ocean and the Persian Gulf, reaching as far as Somalia and Kenya on the eastern coast of Africa.

Post-17th-century Changes

Kangxi (r. 1661-1722), the most renowned emperor of the Qing Dynasty (1644-1911), restored the central empire's rule over Taiwan, and resisted incursions by Tsarist Russia. To reinforce the administration of Tibet, he formulated the rules on the confirmation of the Tibetan local leaders by the Central Government. He effectively administered more than 11 million sq km of Chinese territory.

But during the early 19th century the Qing Dynasty declined rapidly. Britain smuggled large quantities of opium into China, leading to the Qing government imposing a ban on the drug. To protect its opium trade, Britain launched a war of aggression against China in 1840, forcing the Qing government to sign the Treaty of Nanking, a treaty of national humiliation. Many countries, including Britain, the US, France, Russia and Japan, coerced the Qing government to sign various unequal treaties, cede territory and pay reparations following the Opium War. China was gradually relegated to the status of a semi-colonial, semi-feudal country.

Sun Yat-sen

The Revolution of 1911 led by Dr. Sun Yat-sen (1866-1925) was one of the greatest events in modern Chinese history, as it overthrew the Qing Dynasty that had ruled for some 270 years, ended over 2,000 years of feudal monarchy, and founded the Republic of China.

The May 4th Movement of 1919 marked the introduction of Marxism to China. The Communist Party of China (CPC) was founded in the wake of this, in 1921. The new-democratic revolution the CPC led went through four stages, namely the Northern Expeditionary War (1924-1927), the Agrarian Revolutionary War (1927-1937), the War of Resistance Against Japanese Aggression (1937-1945) and the War of Liberation (1945-1949). After the CPC-Kuomintang cooperative victory in the war against the Japanese invaders, the Kuomintang triggered the civil war in 1945. With great efforts during the three years of civil war, the CPC toppled the Kuomintang government in 1949.

The People's Republic of China (PRC) was founded on October 1, 1949.

Soon after its founding, the People's Republic completed the agrarian reform in the areas where 90 percent of China's agricultural population lived, allotting a total of 47 million ha of land to 300 million farmers.

The Third Plenary Session of the 11th CPC Central Committee in 1978 marked a new era for China. Under the lead of Deng Xiaoping (1904-1997), China adopted the "reform and opening up" policy, transferring the focus to a drive to modernize China.

Through its efforts over the past six decades, the ruling Communist Party of China has succeeded in bringing about a stable political situation with economic prosperity, sufficient food and clothing, and active diplomatic engagement, to the most populous developing country in the world.

The Bird's Nest (National Stadium) and the Water Cube (National Aquatics Center) were opened to the public after the 2008 Summer Olympics.

The Path of Chinese History

From the founding of the first state in Chinese history to the reform and opening up era in present-day China, great changes have taken place in this country. Below, we sketch Chinese history chronologically and highlight some key events to discover the country's development path.

● Xia Dynasty (2070 BC-1600 BC)

◇ The First State in Chinese History

The tribal societies of primitive China adopted a power transfer system in which the ruler voluntarily abdicated and selected a worthy man to succeed him in managing tribal affairs. The three famous tribal leaders in the Yellow River region – Yao, Shun and Yu – accomplished power transfer in this way. Upon Yu's death, his son Qi proclaimed himself king, marking the replacement of the old power transfer system by a hereditary system. The first state in Chinese history, the Xia Dynasty, was thus established. It ruled for over 400 years. In 1600 BC, the Xia Dynasty was overthrown and the Shang Dynasty was set up.

● Shang Dynasty (1600 BC-1046 BC)

◇ Oracle Bone Inscription

In the early 20th century archeologists discovered nearly 100,000 pieces of tortoise shells and cattle bones in the ruins of Yin, capital of the Shang Dynasty, in Anyang, Henan Province. These shells and bones are inscribed with nearly 5,000 different characters, recording various Shang activities, such as worship of ancestors and deities, wars and battles, appointment of officials, construction of cities and fortune telling by divination. The oracle bone inscriptions are the earliest evidence of the Chinese written language discovered so far.

● Zhou Dynasty (1046 BC-256 BC)

◇ All Schools of Thought Contending

The period of over 400 years from the 7th to the 3rd centuries BC was the classical era in Chinese philosophy. This epoch witnessed the creation of the main bodies of Chinese philosophy, namely Confucianism, Legalism and Taoism, as well as dozens of other schools of thought, including those of the Military Strategists, Mohism and the Theory of the Five Elements. Confucius and his *Lun Yu* (*Analects*), Lao Zi and his *Dao De Jing* (*Classic of the Way and Virtue*), and Sun Wu and his *Bing Fa* (*Art of War*) are the most representative of this era.

● Qin Dynasty (221 BC-206 BC)

◇ The First United Empire

In 221 BC Qin Shi Huang united China and set up the Qin Dynasty. Qin Shi Huang standardized the written script, weights and measures, and currency, and established the system of prefectures and counties, as well as the system of regulations and decrees. The feudal governmental structure established by him was subsequently followed for over 2,000 years. The emperor initiated the building of the Great Wall, the thoroughfare leading to the northern grassland and his own huge mausoleum. Such a big empire was difficult to rule, and the Qin Dynasty lasted only 15 years before it was replaced by the Han Dynasty.

● Han Dynasty (206 BC-AD 220)

◇ Zhang Qian's Two Diplomatic Missions to the Western Regions

Emperor Wu (156 BC-87 BC) of the Han Dynasty did much to improve the national strength and extended the Silk Road to the Western Regions (A Han Dynasty term for the area west of the Yumen Pass, including what is now Xinjiang and parts of Central Asia – *tr.*) and even as far as Europe, pushing the Han Empire to its apex. He dispatched Zhang Qian (?-114 BC) as imperial envoy to Dayuezhi, an ancient tribal state in the Western Regions, in 138 BC. In 119 BC Zhang Qian went to the Western Regions for the second time. Zhang's two missions strengthened the contacts between the Han people of the Central Plains and the peoples of Central Asia, and ensured smooth trading activities along the Silk Road.

◇ First General History of China

China's first general history, *Shi Ji* (*Records of the Historian*) was completed around 100 BC. The book records Chinese history from the era of the legendary Yellow Emperor to 122 BC, initiating a writing style of presenting history in the form of a series of biographies. The author Sima Qian (c.145 BC-87 BC) laid the groundwork for the work of all subsequent historians.

CHINA

◇ **Invention of the Papermaking**

In 105 Cai Lun (?-121), a eunuch of the Han Dynasty, invented a technique of making paper from tree bark, fishnets, rags and hemp. Such paper was well suited for writing, and its raw materials were cheap and easily came by, facilitating the spread of writing in China and around the world.

● **Three Kingdoms Period (220-280)**

● **Jin Dynasty (265-420)**

● **Northern and Southern Dynasties (420-589)**

◇ **Zu Chongzhi**

Zu Chongzhi (429-500) was an outstanding Chinese mathematician. He was the first person in history to calculate an approximation of the ratio of a circle's circumference to its diameter (π) to seven correct decimal digits. His work of mathematics, *Zhui Shu* (*Method of Interpolation*), served as a text book of the National School of the Tang Dynasty (618-907). He also compiled the Daming calendar that tracked the precession of the equinoxes for the first time.

● **Sui Dynasty (581-618)**

◇ **Grand Canal**

After the Han Dynasty, China was ruled successively by the Three Kingdoms, Jin Dynasty and Northern and Southern Dynasties. This was a period of constant division. It was the Sui Dynasty that united China again.

The construction of the Grand Canal started in 605, during the reign of Sui Dynasty Emperor Yang. He drafted millions of peasants for the work, and completed this canal linking China's north and south within six years. The canal was built on the basis of natural rivers and old canals. Divided into the Yongji, Tongji, Hangou and Jiangnan sections from Zhuojun in the north to Luoyang in the center and to Yuhang in the south, the canal stretched for some 2,000 km. Its construction greatly promoted the transportation and economic exchanges between north and south China.

● **Tang Dynasty (618-907)**

◇ **Princess Wencheng in Tibet**

The Sui Dynasty was succeeded by that of the Tang. In 641 Emperor Taizong married his daughter Princess Wencheng

(625-680) to Songtsen Gampo (?-650), King of Tubo (now Tibet). She showed extraordinary political genius in assisting Songtsen Gampo in governing Tubo and preserving peace between the Tang Dynasty and that kingdom, thus winning the respect of the Tibetan people. When she went to Tubo, she brought many scholars, musicians and agricultural technicians with her, as well as large quantities of tools. Later, she introduced the techniques of rearing silkworms and making wine and paper to the Tibetan people. As a result, both cultural and economic development advanced rapidly in the region.

◇ Jianzhen in Japan

Jianzhen (688-763), an eminent monk of the Tang Dynasty, at the age of 14 was initiated into the Lü (Vinaya) sect of Buddhism. In the year 753 he was invited by a Japanese monastery to preach there. He took with him advanced Chinese knowledge of architecture, sculpture, painting and medicine.

● Song Dynasty (960-1279)

◇ Invention of Movable-type Printing

The Song Dynasty was another era when China was united again after the Tang Dynasty. It lasted over 300 years under the reign of 16 emperors. During this dynasty, handcrafts developed rapidly, while remarkable technical innovations were made in the fields of mining and metallurgy, textiles, porcelain making, shipbuilding, and papermaking.

Bi Sheng (?-c. 1051) invented movable-type printing. He carved individual characters on clay cubes and heated them into pottery. The pottery types were arranged within an iron frame. Printing and typesetting could proceed at the same time, and the pottery types could be reused repeatedly. Movable-type printing is considered a major revolution in the printing history of humankind.

● Yuan Dynasty (1271-1368)

◇ Beijing-Hangzhou Grand Canal

The Yuan Dynasty was established by the Mongols, who vanquished the Song Dynasty. In order to increase grain transportation and enhance economic and cultural exchanges between north and south China, the Yuan excavated a direct north-south waterway linking Beijing and Hangzhou based on the track of earlier canals and natural waterways. Extending for 1,794 km, the canal connects the Hai, Yellow, Huai, Yangtze and Qiantang river systems.

Ming Dynasty (1368-1644)

Zheng He's Seven Voyages

In 1368 Zhu Yuanzhang, a leader of the Red Turban rebels, overthrew the Yuan Dynasty and established the Ming Dynasty. In the space of two centuries the Ming made great achievements in economy, culture, science and technology. Not long after the dynasty was established, Zheng He (1371-1435), a eunuch, was assigned by the central authorities to lead huge fleets to explore the Western Seas on seven voyages from 1405 to 1433. They passed through 30 countries and reached as far as the east coast of Africa and the Red Sea estuary. The voyages promoted economic exchanges between China and other Asian countries, and Africa.

Qing Dynasty (1644-1911)

Recapture of Taiwan by Zheng Chenggong

The Qing Dynasty was the last feudal regime in China. In 1616 the Manchu people in northeast China set up their khanate, and in 1644 entered the Central Plains through the Shanhai Pass and replaced the Ming Dynasty. Zheng Chenggong (1624-1662), a Ming Dynasty general, organized a big fleet in southeastern China and resisted the Qing conquest until 1662, when he retreated to Taiwan with over 20,000 men and several hundred ships.

At the time the Dutch East India Company had occupied Taiwan and made it a trading colony. Zheng Chenggong fought the Dutch troops and recaptured Taiwan and the Penghu Islands (called Pescadores by the Portuguese), reestablishing Chinese sovereignty there. In 1684 the Qing government set up, under its direct control, Taiwan Prefecture, and later Taiwan Province.

Establishment of Dalai and Panchen Titles

In 1653 Qing Emperor Shunzhi officially confirmed the title of Dalai Lama on the Fifth Dalai. In 1713 Qing Emperor Kangxi dispatched an envoy to confirm the title of Panchen

Erdeni on the Fifth Panchen. The Qing court also stipulated that the Dalai Lama and the Panchen Erdeni of later generations must be authorized by the Central Government. This system has been maintained to the present day.

◇ First Opium War

Britain forced China to open its doors by smuggling opium into China in the early 19th century. Chinese official Lin Zexu burned nearly 1.2 million kg of opium in public at Humen, Guangdong, in 1839. On June 28, 1840 a British naval fleet blocked the mouth of the Pearl River, seized Xiamen, Shanghai and other ports, and sailed up the Yangtze River to attack Nanjing.

◇ Treaty of Nanking

On August 29, 1842, when British troops arrived at the city walls of Nanjing, the Qing government was forced to sign the unequal Treaty of Nanking. According to the Treaty, China had to cede Hong Kong to Britain and open up five treaty ports, as well as pay huge sums in reparations. The US, France, Spain and Italy, in succession, obtained the same privileges by force. China was hence relegated to being a semi-colony of the Western powers.

◇ Second Opium War

From 1856 to 1860 the British and French allied fleet, supported by Russia and the US, launched the Second Opium War on China and forced the Qing government to sign more unequal treaties with the four countries. Apart from enormous amounts in reparations, China lost large areas of territory. Yuanmingyuan (Garden of Perfection and Brightness) in Beijing, known as the "garden of gardens," was destroyed by the British and French allied forces.

◇ Westernization Movement

The Westernization Movement, which thrived from the 1860s to the mid-1890s, was initiated by the Qing government to learn from Western capitalist countries in respect of military, political, economic, cultural and diplomatic techniques. The activities included setting up military industry and related enterprises, equipping the army and navy with new-type weapons, and dispatching Chinese students to study in Europe and North America. The Movement was intended to make China strong and prosperous, but ended in failure.

CHINA

◇ Sino-French War

In 1883 French colonists provoked a war on the border of China and Vietnam. In the following year French troops attacked Qing troops in Lang Son in Vietnam and the Chinese fleets in Taiwan and Fujian provinces. The Sino-French War unfolded in Taiwan and Vietnam at the same time. The French troops were defeated, and consequently the French cabinet fell from power. The Qing government could have won a victory, but it signed a truce agreement with France in 1885 – the Treaty of Tientsin. China lost an important fleet in the southeast coast, while France was able to infiltrate China's Yunnan, Guangxi and Kwangchowan.

◇ Sino-Japanese War 1894-1895

In 1894 Japan invaded Korea and China, and Chinese soldiers and civilians fought back, resulting in the First Sino-Japanese War. Soon the Japanese troops controlled the Korean Peninsula, took command of the sea after battles in the Yellow Sea, and then attacked China's northeastern cities and coastal cities in Shandong, defeated China's Beiyang Fleet. In 1895 the two sides signed the Treaty of Shimonoseki, which imposed heavy debts on the Chinese government and reduced China further to a semi-colonial and semi-feudal society. China's Diaoyu Islands were also captured by Japan during the war.

◇ Reform Movement

In 1898 Kang Youwei (1858-1927), together with others, started a reform movement involving political, military, economic and cultural changes. They dreamed of establishing a constitutional monarchy with the support of the Qing government, to make the country strong and prosperous. The movement encountered stiff resistance from royal conservatives and, after lasting 100 days, was ended by a cruel massacre.

● Republic of China (1912-1949)

◇ Revolution of 1911

The Revolution of 1911 was a democratic revolution led by Sun Yat-sen. In 1911, when the Qing government planned to give the authority for railway construction in China to foreign companies, forces from all quarters united to rise up and seize political power in the southern provinces.

On January 1, 1912, the provisional government of the Republic of China was founded in Nanjing. On February 12 the last Qing emperor was forced to abdicate, and the 2,000-year feudal monarchy was replaced with a republic.

◇ May 4th Movement

The May 4th Movement of 1919 is regarded the ideological origin of many important events in modern Chinese history. Its direct cause was an unequal treaty imposed on China after World War I. Motivated by strong patriotism, students initiated the movement, which further developed into a national protest involving people from all sectors of society. It also marked the introduction to China of various new ideologies, among which the spread of Marxism is especially noteworthy.

◇ Birth of the CPC

In 1921 a body of 13 delegates including Mao Zedong (1893-1976), representing communist groups throughout the country, held the First National Congress in Shanghai to found the Communist Party of China (CPC). Today's CPC, with over 85 million members, is the mainstay of Chinese society. Mao Zedong, one of the founders of the CPC and the People's Republic of China, made extraordinary contributions to China's revolution and construction. He was a revolutionary and strategist, as well as a poet and calligrapher.

◇ War of Resistance Against Japanese Aggression

From 1937 to 1945 the Chinese people struggled doggedly against the aggression of Japanese imperialism, and won the final victory in what is known as the War of Resistance Against

Japanese Aggression. Chinese military and civilian casualties exceeded 35 million; and China's direct economic losses, from 1937 figures converted to current value, surpassed US$100 billion, with indirect losses of over US$500 billion, as well as the loss of incalculably precious cultural heritage items.

● People's Republic of China (1949-)

◇ Founding of the People's Republic

On October 1, 1949, a grand ceremony witnessed by crowds of people was held on the Tiananmen Square in Beijing. At the ceremony Mao Zedong, chairman of the Central People's Government, solemnly proclaimed the founding of the People's Republic of China.

◇ First Five-year Plan

The First Five-year Plan (1953-1957) accomplished great achievements: the average annual increase rate of national income reached 8.9 percent or higher; a number of basic industries necessary for national industrialization, until then non-existent domestically, were established, including ones for producing airplanes, automobiles, heavy and precision machinery, power-generating equipment, metallurgical and mining equipment, high-grade alloy steels and non-ferrous metals.

From that time on, the Chinese government has set economic objectives for every five years. The 12th Five-year Plan (2011-2015) is now under way.

◇ Reform and Opening Up

The Third Plenary Session of the 11th CPC Central Committee, held at the end of 1978, ushered in a new historic era for China. Chinese leader Deng Xiaoping vigorously promoted the policy of reform and opening up, and placed the national work focus on modernization. A road to modernization with Chinese characteristics was gradually established, through opening up and reforms in the economic, political and cultural structures.

In 1992 Deng Xiaoping, the principal architect of China's reform and opening up, during a southern inspection tour made some important speeches, collectively regarded as key endorsement for economic reform and social progress in the following years.

Jiang Zemin and Hu Jintao became General Secretary of the CPC Central Committee in 1989 and in 2002, respectively. They inherited and developed the policy of reform and opening up initiated by Deng Xiaoping, and respectively put forth the important thought of Three Represents and the Scientific Outlook on Development, with the result that China attained rapid economic growth and remarkable improvement in its standard of living.

In 2012 Xi Jinping was elected as the new General Secretary of the CPC Central Committee.

◇ Return of Hong Kong and Macao to China

China resumed its exercise of sovereignty over Hong Kong on July 1, 1997, and over Macao on December 20, 1999, establishing Hong Kong Special Administrative Region and Macao Special Administrative Region, respectively. The Central Government applies the basic policies of "one country, two systems" and a high degree of autonomy to the two places. "One country, two systems" refers to the fact that in China, a unified country, the mainland practices the socialist system, while Hong Kong and Macao retain their original capitalist system and way of life unchanged for 50 years.

CHINA

A Brief Chronology of Chinese History

	Xia Dynasty	c. 2070 BC–c. 1600 BC
	Shang Dynasty	c. 1600 BC–1046 BC
Zhou Dynasty 1046 BC–256 BC	Western Zhou	1046 BC–771 BC
	Eastern Zhou: Spring and Autumn Period (770 BC–476 BC); Warring States Period (475 BC–221 BC)	770 BC–256 BC
	Qin Dynasty	221 BC–206 BC
Han Dynasty 206 BC–AD 220	Western Han (including the short-lived Xin Dynasty and Emperor Gengshi)	206 BC–AD 25
	Eastern Han	25–220
Three Kingdoms 220–280	Wei	220–265
	Shu Han	221–263
	Wu	222–280
Jin Dynasty 265–420	Western Jin	265–317
	Eastern Jin	317–420
Northern and Southern Dynasties 420–589	Southern Dynasties 420–589 — Song	420–479
	Qi	479–502
	Liang	502–557
	Chen	557–589

	Northern Dynasties 386-581	Northern Wei	386-534
		Eastern Wei	534-550
		Northern Qi	550-577
		Western Wei	535-556
		Northern Zhou	557-581
Sui Dynasty			581-618
Tang Dynasty			618-907
Five Dynasties 907-960	Later Liang		907-923
	Later Tang		923-936
	Later Jin		936-947
	Later Han		947-950
	Later Zhou		951-960
Song Dynasty 960-1279	Northern Song		960-1127
	Southern Song		1127-1279
Liao Dynasty			907-1125
Kin Dynasty			1115-1234
Yuan Dynasty			1271-1368
Ming Dynasty			1368-1644
Qing Dynasty			1644-1911
Republic of China			1912-1949
People's Republic of China			October 1, 1949-

中 国 China

China is divided into 23 provinces, five autonomous regions, four municipalities directly under the Central Government and two special administrative regions. Since the policy of reform and opening up was introduced in 1978, the country's rapid economic development has brought about an accelerating process of urbanization. An onerous task for China in the 21st century is how to promote the urbanization process in a positive and stable way.

Administrative Divisions

- Administrative Divisions
- Brief Descriptions of Provinces and Provincial-level Municipalities and Autonomous Regions
- The Road to New-type Urbanization

CHINA

Forbidden City, the imperial palaces of the Ming and Qing dynasties, Beijing

Administrative Divisions

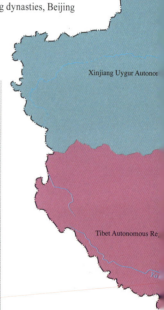

North China: Beijing Tianjin Hebei Province Shanxi Province
Inner Mongolia Autonomous Region
Northeast: Liaoning Province Jilin Province
Heilongjiang Province
East China: Shanghai Jiangsu Province Zhejiang Province
Anhui Province Fujian Province Jiangxi Province
Shandong Province
Central South: Henan Province Hubei Province Hunan Province
Guangdong Province Hainan Province
Guangxi Zhuang Autonomous Region
Southwest: Chongqing Sichuan Province Guizhou Province
Yunan Province Tibet Autonomous Region
Northwest: Shaanxi Province Gansu Province Qinghai Province
Ningxia Hui Autonomous Region
Xijiang Uygur Autonomous Region

Hong Kong Special Administrative Region
Macao Special Administrative Region
Taiwan Province

Legend

★ Capital   ⊙ Provincial-level administrative center

⌐⌐⌐ National border   ⌐⌐⌐ Undefined national border

--- Boundary lines of provinces,
autonomous regions and municipalities

--- Boundary lines of special administrative regions

Administrative Divisions 041

Brief Descriptions of Provinces and Provincial-level Municipalities and Autonomous Regions

1 Beijing

Land area	16,800 sq km
Population	21.148 million
Population density	1,259 people/sq km
Average life expectancy	81.12
Regional GDP	RMB1,950 billion
Main farm products	Vegetables, fruit
Arable land area	231,700 ha
Main industries	Telecommunications, electronics
Railways	1,228.4 km
Highways	21,614km
Main mineral resources	Coal, iron, limestone
Exports	US$63.25 billion
College students (per m. people)	55,340
Annual inbound tourists	4.501 million
Motor vehicles	5.437 million

2 Tianjin

Land area	11,300 sq km
Population	13.546 million
Population density	1,100 people/sq km
Average life expectancy	80.65
Regional GDP	RMB 1,437.016 billion
Main farm products	Wheat, corn and rice
Arable land area	441,100 ha
Main industries	Oil products, textile
Railways	866.9 km
Highways	15,163 km
Main mineral resources	Chambersite, manganese, gold
Exports	US$44.498 billion
College students (per m. people)	43,580
Annual inbound tourists	730,600
Tianjin Port's throughput	453 million tons

3 Hebei

Land area	187,700 sq km
Population	73.326 million
Population density	391 people/sq km
Average life expectancy	73.4
Regional GDP	RMB 2,830.14 billion
Main farm products	Wheat, corn, bean, fruit
Arable land area	6,317,300 ha
Main industries	Iron and steel, equipment, petrochemicals
Railways	5,170.5 km
Highways	174,000 km
Main mineral resources	34 minerals among top 5 in China
Exports	US$30.96 billion
College students (per m. people)	20,630
Annual inbound tourists	1.338 million
Minerals with confirmed reserves	125 kinds

4 Shanxi

Land area	156,000 sq km
Population	36.3 million
Population density	233 people/sq km
Average life expectancy	73.49
Regional GDP	RMB 1,260.22 billion
Main farm products	Wheat, corn, cotton
Arable land area	4,055,800 ha
Main industries	Coal, metallurgy
Railways	3,773.7 km
Highways	139,000 km
Main mineral resources	Coal, iron, bauxite
Exports	US$8 billion
College students (per m. people)	23,510
Annual inbound tourists	2.126 million
Coal reserves	267.379 billion tons

5 Inner Mongolia

Land area	1,197,500 sq km
Population	24.817 million
Population density	20 people/sq km
Average life expectancy	71
Regional GDP	RMB 1,424.611 billion
Main farm products	Wheat, beet, animal husbandry
Arable land area	7,147,200 ha
Main industries	Coal, iron and steel, metallurgy
Railways	9,161.9 km
Highways	160,995 km
Main mineral resources	Rare earth, coal, silver
Exports	US$4.687 billion
College students (per m. people)	20,420
Annual inbound tourists	1.515 million
Grassland area	86.667 million ha

6 Liaoning

Land area	145,900 sq km
Population	43.9 million
Population density	301 people/sq km
Average life expectancy	75.6
Regional GDP	RMB 2,707.77 billion
Main farm products	Rice, wheat, corn, soybean
Arable land area	4,085,300 ha
Main industries	Aeronautics, automobiles, iron and steel, equipment
Railways	4,867.4 km
Highways	110,072 km
Main mineral resources	Iron, manganese, oil, gas
Exports	US$64.54 billion
College students (per m. people)	28,110
Annual inbound tourists	5.031 million
Industrial added value	RMB 1,251.03 billion

7 Jilin

Land area	187,400 sq km
Population	27.494 million
Population density	147 people/sq km
Average life expectancy	73.9
Regional GDP	RMB 1,298.146 billion
Main farm products	Rice, soybean, corn, potato
Arable land area	5,534,600 ha
Main industries	Automobiles, equipment
Railways	4,222 km
Highways	94,200 km
Main mineral resources	Oil shale, diatomite
Exports	US$6.757 billion
College students (per m. people)	28,890
Annual inbound tourists	1.274 million
Height of Heavenly Lake on Mt Changbai	2,189.1 m

8 Heilongjiang

Land area	460,000 sq km
Population	38.34 million
Population density	83 people/sq km
Average life expectancy	73
Regional GDP	RMB 1,250.38 billion
Main farm product	Wheat, soybean, beet
Arable land area	11,830,100 ha
Main industries	Equipment, machinery, petrochemicals
Railways	5,945.3 km
Highways	155,592 km
Main mineral resources	Coal, oil, gold
Exports	US$17.67 billion
College students (per m. people)	24,410
Annual inbound tourists	2.065 million
Total grain output	55.706 million tons

9 Shanghai

Land area	6,340.5 sq km
Population	24.151 million
Population density	3,809 people/sq km
Average life expectancy	82.51
Regional GDP	RMB 2,160.212 billion
Main farm products	Rice, rapeseed, fish
Arable land area	244,000 ha
Main industries	Comprehensive industries
Railways	461.3 km
Highways	12,084 km
Main mineral resources	Subsea oil and gas
Exports	US$204.244 billion
College students (per m. people)	34,810
Annual inbound tourists	7.574 million
Average commuting time	47 minutes

10 Jiangsu

Land area	102,600 sq km
Population	79.395 million
Population density	774 people/sq km
Average life expectancy	76.63
Regional GDP	RMB 5,916.18 billion
Main farm products	Rice, rapeseed, silkworm, fish
Arable land area	4,763,800 ha
Main industries	Machinery, electronics, textiles, silk
Railways	2,554.1 km
Highways	156,000 km
Main mineral resources	Calcite, marlstone
Exports	US$328.85 billion
College students (per m. people)	27,860
Annual inbound tourists	2.88 million
Lakes of more than 50 sq km	12

11 Zhejiang

Land area	101,800 sq km
Population	54.98 million
Population density	540 people/sq km
Average life expectancy	77
Regional GDP	RMB 3,756.8 billion
Main farm products	Rice, tea, silkworms, aquatic products
Arable land area	1,920,900 ha
Main industries	Medicine, chemical fibers, silk
Railways	1,779.1 km
Highways	111,776 km
Main mineral resources	Stone coal, alum
Exports	US$248.8 billion
College students (per m. people)	22,880
Annual inbound tourists	8.66 million
Length of Qiantang River	668 km

12 Anhui

Land area	139,600 sq km
Population	60.298 million
Population density	432 people/sq km
Average life expectancy	74
Regional GDP	RMB 1,903.89 billion
Main farm products	Rice, wheat, cotton, tea
Arable land area	5,730,200 ha
Main industries	Coal, metallurgy, textile, foodstuff
Railways	3,443 km
Highways	149,535 km
Main mineral resources	Coal, iron, copper, sulfur
Exports	US$28.25 billion
College students (per m. people)	21,010
Annual inbound tourists	3.855 million
Mt Huangshan tourist resort area	160.6 sq km

13 Fujian

Land area	121,400 sq km
Population	37.74 million
Population density	311 people/sq km
Average life expectancy	73.8
Regional GDP	RMB 2,175.964 billion
Main farm products	Fruit, flower
Arable land area	1,330,100 ha
Main industries	Shipping, hydropower
Railways	2,743 km
Highways	99,535 km
Main mineral resources	Quartz sand
Exports	US$106.504 billion
College students (per m. people)	23,010
Annual inbound tourists	5.121 million
Length of Zheng He's voyages to the Western Seas	Over 130,000 sea miles

14 Jiangxi

Land area	166,900 sq km
Population	45.222 million
Population density	271 people/sq km
Average life expectancy	74.33
Regional GDP	RMB 1,433.85 billion
Main farm products	Rice, oilseed, fish
Arable land area	2,827,100 ha
Main industries	Machinery, electronics
Railways	2,834.5 km
Highways	146,632 km
Main mineral resources	Copper, tungsten, gold, silver
Exports	US$28.17 billion
College students (per m. people)	22,950
Annual inbound tourists	1.636 million
Height of Prince Teng's Pavilion	57.5 m

15 Shandong

Land area	156,700 sq km
Population	97.334 million
Population density	622 people/sq km
Average life expectancy	75
Regional GDP	RMB 5,468.43 billion
Main farm products	Wheat, corn, peanut, fruit
Arable land area	7,515,300 ha
Main industries	Energy, foodstuff, chemicals, power
Railways	4,200.3 km
Highways	233,190 km
Main mineral resources	Gold, coal, oil
Exports	US$134.51 billion
College students (per m. people)	22,380
Annual inbound tourists	4.242 million
Height of Mt Tai	1,545 m

16 Henan

Land area	167,000 sq km
Population	106.01 million
Population density	635 people/sq km
Average life expectancy	73
Regional GDP	RMB 3,215.586 billion
Main farm products	Wheat, corn, cotton
Arable land area	7,926,400 ha
Main industries	Foodstuff, machinery
Railways	5,165 km
Highways	247,587 km
Main mineral resources	Molybdenum, kyanite
Exports	US$35.992 billion
College students (per m. people)	20,120
Annual inbound tourists	2.073 million
Number of oracle characters	4,500

17 Hubei

Land area	185,900 sq km
Population	57.99 million
Population density	312 people/sq km
Average life expectancy	75.86
Regional GDP	RMB 2,466.849 billion
Main farm products	Rice, wheat, cotton, oilseed
Arable land area	4,664,100 ha
Main industries	Iron and steel, machinery
Railways	3,354.9 km
Highways	212,747 km
Main mineral resources	Phosphonium, rutile, wolllastonite
Exports	US$22.838 billion
College students (per m. people)	30,780
Annual inbound tourists	2.68 million
Capacity of Three Gorges Reservoir	39.3 billion m^3

18 Hunan

Land area	211,800 sq km
Population	66.906 million
Population density	316 people/sq km
Average life expectancy	74.7
Regional GDP	RMB 2,450.17 billion
Main farm products	Rice, ramee, tobacco
Arable land area	3,789,400 ha
Main industries	Metallurgy, machinery
Railways	3,696.3 km
Highways	235,000 km
Main mineral resources	Tungsten, bismuth
Exports	US$14.82 billion
College students (per m. people)	20,870
Annual inbound tourists	2.307 million
Number. of generals from Hunan	6

19 Guangdong

Land area	178,000 sq km
Population	106.44 million
Population density	598 people/sq km
Average life expectancy	76.1
Regional GDP	RMB 6,216.397 billion
Main farm products	Rice, sugarcane, peanut, fruit
Arable land area	2,830,700 ha
Main industries	Electronics, home appliance
Railways	2,832.1 km
Highways	202,900 km
Main mineral resources	Kaolin and peat soil
Exports	US$636.404 billion
College students (per m. people)	20,820
Annual inbound tourists	101.106 million
Import and export throughput	454.03 million tons

20 Guangxi

Land area	237,700 sq km
Population	51.99 million
Population density	219 people/sq km
Average life expectancy	73.29
Regional GDP	RMB 1,171.435 billion
Main farm products	Sugarcane, tobacco, cassava
Arable land area	4,217,500 ha
Main industries	Sugar refining
Railways	3,194.2 km
Highways	104,889 km
Main mineral resources	Indium, manganese, tin
Exports	US$12.459 billion
College students (per m. people)	18,340
Annual inbound tourists	3.028 million
Karst area	70,000 ha

21 Hainan

Land area	35,000 sq km
Population	8.953 million
Population density	256 people/sq km
Average life expectancy	74
Regional GDP	RMB 314.646 billion
Main farm products	Rice, sugarcane, rubber
Arable land area	727,500 ha
Main industries	Light and chemical industries
Railways	693.7 km
Highways	22,916 km
Main mineral resources	Silica
Exports	US$3.706 billion
College students (per m. people)	22,180
Annual inbound tourists	756,400
Fruit output	4.029 million tons

22 Chongqing

Land area	82,300 sq km
Population	29.7 million
Population density	361 people/sq km
Average life expectancy	76.58
Regional GDP	RMB 1,265.669 billion
Main farm products	Rice, wheat, rapeseed, tea
Arable land area	2,235,900 ha
Main industries	Automobiles, medicine, foodstuff
Railways	1,373.4 km
Highways	122,800 km
Main mineral resources	Strontium, manganese, vanadium
Exports	US$46.797 billion
College students (per m. people)	27,340
Annual inbound tourists	2.423 million
Hydraulic power capacity	7.5 million KW

23 Sichuan

Land area	485,000 sq km
Population	81.07 million
Population density	168 people/sq km
Average life expectancy	74.75
Regional GDP	RMB 2,626.08 billion
Main farm products	Rice, cotton, oilseed, silk
Arable land area	5,947,400 ha
Main industries	Metallurgy, chemical and textile industries, foodstuff
Railways	3,518 km
Highways	283,268 km
Main mineral resources	Vanadium, titanium, calcium
Exports	US$41.95 billion
College students (per m. people)	20,370
Annual inbound tourists	2.096 million
Rare animals	55 species

24 Guizhou

Land area	176,100 sq km
Population	35.022 million
Population density	199 people/sq km
Average life expectancy	71.1
Regional GDP	RMB 800.679 billion
Main farm products	Rice, tobacco, tung tree
Arable land area	4,485,300 ha
Main industries	Water conservancy, mining
Railways	2,093 km
Highways	169,700 km
Main mineral resources	Mercury, barite
Exports	US$6.886 billion
College students (per m. people)	13,920
Annual inbound tourists	777,000
Width of Huangguoshu Waterfall	101 m

25 Yunnan

Land area	394,000 sq km
Population	46.31 million
Population density	117 people/sq km
Average life expectancy	70.09
Regional GDP	RMB 875.095 billion
Main farm products	Rice, corn, flower, tobacco
Arable land area	6,072,100 ha
Main industries	Light industry, power, foodstuff
Railways	2,491.3 km
Highways	214,524 km
Main mineral resources	Copper, tin
Exports	US$9.473 billion
College students (per m. people)	15,660
Annual inbound tourists	3.954 million
Number of stone bridges in Lijiang	354

26 Tibet

Land area	1,274,900 sq km
Population	3.002 million
Population density	2.36 people/sq km
Average life expectancy	67
Regional GDP	RMB 60.583 billion
Main farm products	Rice, highland barley
Arable land area	361,600 ha
Main industries	Cement, Tibetan medicine
Railways	531.5 km
Highways	63,108 km
Main mineral resources	Copper, lithium
Exports	US$1.183 billion
College students (per m. people)	15,080
Annual inbound tourists	270,800
Number of preserved temples	More than 1,700

27 Shaanxi

Land area	205,600 sq km
Population	37.637 million
Population density	183 people/sq km
Average life expectancy	72.5
Regional GDP	RMB 1,604.521 billion
Main farm products	Rice, wheat, beans
Arable land area	4,050,300 ha
Main industries	Coal, oil, gas
Railways	4,083.4 km
Highways	151,986 km
Main mineral resources	Coal, oil, gas
Exports	US$10.224 billion
College students (per m. people)	35,250
Annual inbound tourists	3.521 million
Number of historic sites	36,000

28 Gansu

Land area	454,400 sq km
Population	25.822 million
Population density	57 people/sq km
Average life expectancy	72.23
Regional GDP	RMB 626.8 billion
Main farm products	Wheat, corn, flax
Arable land area	4,658,800 ha
Main industries	Nonferrous metal, petrochemicals
Railways	2,441.5 km
Highways	123,696 km
Main mineral resources	Coal, oil, gas
Exports	US$4.679 billion
College students (per m. people)	21,450
Annual inbound tourists	97,700
Area of Dunhuang murals	45,000 sq m

29 Qinghai

Land area	721,200 sq km
Population	5.778 million
Population density	8 people/sq km
Average life expectancy	69.96
Regional GDP	RMB 210.105 billion
Main farm products	Wheat, highland barley, rapeseed
Arable land area	542,700 ha
Main industries	Electricity, crude oil, crude salt
Railways	1,856 km
Highways	70,117 km
Main mineral resources	Potassium, sodium, magnesium, lithium
Exports	US$847 million
College students (per m. people)	11,330
Annual inbound tourists	46,500
Area of Qinghai Lake	4,583 sq km

30 Ningxia

Land area	62,800 sq km
Population	6.395 million
Population density	102 people/sq km
Average life expectancy	73.54
Regional GDP	RMB 206.079 billion
Main farm products	Rice, wheat
Arable land area	1,107,100 ha
Main industries	Coal, electricity
Railways	1,266.5 km
Highways	24,506 km
Main mineral resources	Coal, silica, gypsum
Exports	US$1.6 billion
College students (per m. people)	21,070
Annual inbound tourists	19,500
Proportion of Hui ethnic group of Ningxia's population	36%

31 Xinjiang

Land area	1,655,800 sq km
Population	22.643 million
Population density	14 people/sq km
Average life expectancy	72
Regional GDP	RMB 815 billion
Main farm products	Wheat, cotton, flax, fruit, melon
Arable land area	4,124,600 ha
Main industries	Textile, petrolchemicals
Railways	4,911 km
Highways	170,100 km
Main mineral resources	Coal, oil, gas
Exports	US$22.27 billion
College students (per m. people)	15,960
Annual inbound tourists	1.567 million
Area of Tarim Basin	530,000 sq km

Administrative Divisions 051

32 Hong Kong

Land area	1,104.41 sq km
Population	7.22 million
Population density	6,538 people/sq km
Average life expectancy	83.6
Regional GDP	HK$ 2,122.492 billion
Main farm products	Vegetable, flower, fruit
Main industries	Electronics, textile, garment
Railways	175 km
Highways	2,086 km
Main mineral resources	Iron, aluminum, zinc, tungsten
Exports	US$535.55 billion
Registered college students	332,500
Annual inbound tourists	54.299 million
Government supported rental apartments	768,100

33 Macao

Land area	29.9 sq km
Population	607,500
Population density	20,318 people/sq km
Average life expectancy	82.4
Regional GDP	MOP$ 34.822 billion
Main farm products	Vegetable, flower
Main industries	Toy, garment
Highways	309.1 km
Main mineral resource	Granite
Exports	MOP$ 909.39 million
Registered college students	27,776
Annual inbound tourists	29.325 million
Lottery industry revenue	MOP$ 306.49 billion

34 Taiwan

Land area	36,192 sq km
Population	23.305 million
Population density	644 people/sq km
Average life expectancy	79.15
Regional GDP	US$ 474.084 billion
Main farm products	Rice, sugarcane, tea, fruit
Main industries	Textile, electronics, sugar refining
Railways	4,500 km
Highways	40,262 km
Main mineral resources	Gold, copper, oil, gas
Exports	US$ 305.5 billion
Annual inbound tourists	26.29 million
Proportion of education spending in GDP	6.1%

The Road to New-type Urbanization

New-type urbanization

China's urbanization rate in 1978 was 17.9 percent, while this figure reached 52.6 percent in 2012. During the 12th Five-year Plan period (2011-2015), China will be entering a new stage witnessing the double-transformation of urbanization and city development with an estimated urbanization rate increasing by 0.8 to 1.0 percentage point annually and reaching 65 percent in 2030. China, based on its own conditions, has explored a path coordinating development between large and medium-sized cities and small towns.

As a major strategy of China's development, urbanization does not merely mean an increase in the ratio of urban population or expansion of urban areas, but a township-to-city transformation in industrial support, living environment, social security and way of life.

In the face of excessive development of urbanization, the Central Government is, through strategic regional planning, coordinating the relationship between population, land, environment, and economic and social development, and carrying out the policy of "strictly controlling the scale of large cities, properly developing medium-sized cities and actively building small ones." Selected satellite towns are planned to be built around large cities.

The sprawl of urban areas and the explosion of the urban population have triggered problems in the process of urbanization, such as population concentration in downtown areas, traffic congestion, environmental deterioration, soaring land prices and house rents, and employment difficulties. The government has been prioritizing the improvement of residential environment in both urban and rural

Children playing in urban park

Rural community

New community in a county seat

areas, and making considerable progress in housing conditions, coverage rate of green plants, environmental quality and the supply of drinking water.

One of the important tasks for the promotion of urban-rural and regional structural adjustment and coordination of long-term, stable and relatively rapid economic development is balancing the development of big, medium and small cities and realizing the common prosperity of city groups in China's eastern, central and western areas. Various types of urban regional economies with the urban system as the regional framework will soon basically come into being. The pattern of urban regional economy will increasingly improve and the concentration of the urban economy will be further enhanced.

The construction of China's future urbanization will adhere to the three principles of "fairness and sharing," "intensity and high efficiency" and "sustainability," and follow the requirement of depending on large cities and focusing on medium and small cities to gradually form city groups with strong radiating effects and promote the coordinated development of big, medium and small cities and townships to transform the way of urbanization from rapid expansion to quality improvement.

Reform of the Household Registration System

Following the rapid urbanization process, the reform of the household registration management system is also gaining momentum. Some provinces and cities have relaxed their strict control over household registration, creating more opportunities for rural people to migrate to cities.

On February 23, 2012, the General Office of the State Council issued the Notice on Promoting the Household Registration Management System Reform in an Active and Prudent Way, demanding that the downtown areas of county-level cities, seats of county governments and designated towns remove controls over household registration; medium-sized and small cities with districts lift control over household registration to people who have had legal and stable jobs for a certain number of years; and large cities rationally control their population sizes and further improve the present registration policies.

In 2013 the Guangzhou Municipal Public Security Bureau announced that the city had removed agricultural and non-agricultural household discrimination, and unified the registration as "Guangzhou Municipal Residency."

中 国 C h i n a

China is the most populous country in the world, featuring the harmonious coexistence of 56 ethnic groups. The Han ethnic group accounts for the majority of the population and all ethnic groups have merged and live together in large or small scales. *Hanyu* (Chinese language) is the most commonly used language in China and most ethnic-minority groups have their own language. China is also a multi-religious country where various religions coexist.

Population and Ethnicity

- Population
- Ethnic Groups
- Spoken and Written Languages
- Religion

Population

http://www.nhfpc.gov.cn/

At the instruction of the 18th National Congress of the CPC, the National Health and Family Planning Commission was established to be compatible with a new round of the "super-ministry system" reform scheme put forward in 2013 and the Plan for State Council Institutional Reform and Transformation of Government Functions (Draft).

China has 1.339 billion people living on the mainland (according to the sixth national census in 2010), or about one-fifth of the world's total population.

It has a high population density, with more than 140 people per sq km. This population, however, is unevenly distributed. The eastern coastal areas are densely populated, with more than 400 people per sq km; while in the sparsely populated plateaus in the west there are fewer than 10 people per sq km.

Basic contents of family planning: The state encourages late marriage and child-bearing, having fewer but healthier babies, and one child per couple. But a flexible practice is adopted for rural people and ethnic minorities. In rural areas couples may have a second baby in exceptional cases, but must wait several years after the birth of the first child. In areas inhabited by minority peoples, couples may have a second

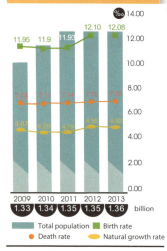

Demographic studies show that in 2011 China's population aged 15 to 64 years surpassed one billion for the first time, to stand at 1,002.83 million, accounting for 74.4 percent of the total population. From 2005 to 2013 the 15-64 population group expanded annually.

Children are the hope of life.

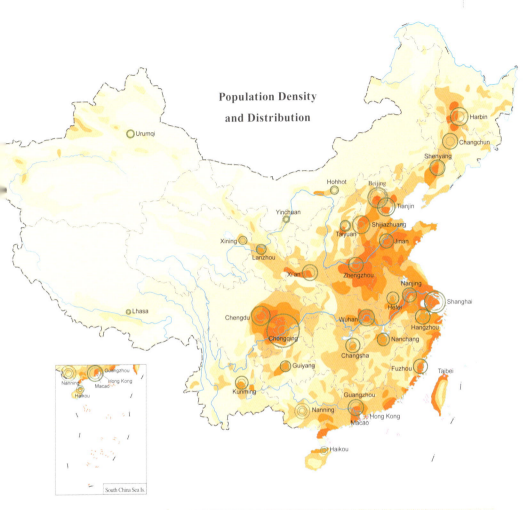

Demographic Dividend

China has achieved sustained and rapid economic growth over the past few decades, which is recognized worldwide as a miracle. In this case, many people give the credit to the demographic dividend, or "population bonus." Unfortunately, figures released by the National Bureau of Statistics show that the number of workers between the ages of 15 and 59 decreased by 3.45 million year on year in 2012, marking the first "absolute decrease" in China's labor force in decades. Obviously, China's demographic dividend is fading, which might lead to a slowdown in its economic growth. Meanwhile, some scholars believe that a new demographic dividend is taking shape as China's growth pattern is changing from one characterized by ordinary skilled workers to one that relies on highly skilled workers.

Population density
(persons per sq km)

- 600 and above
- 400–600
- 100–400
- 50–100
- 1–50
- 0–1

Aging Population

According to the age structure of China's population, the number of people aged from 15 to 64 exceeded one billion in 2011, reaching 1,002.83 million. In 2012 the number further increased to 1,004.03 million, accounting for 74.1 percent of the total population. From 2003 to 2012 the number had kept increasing year by year. It is predicted that the number of people aged above 60 will reach 216 million by 2015, accounting for 16.7 percent of the total population. Population aging will inevitably cause new problems and pressures, and pose new challenges for economic and social development.

In order to tackle this challenge, the Decision passed at the Third Plenary Session of the 18th CPC Central Committee recommended working out a policy to gradual extend the age of retirement and officially launch the policy of allowing a couple to have a second child as long as one of them is the only child of his or her family.

baby, or a third in some places. As for ethnic minorities with extremely small populations, couples may have as many children as they wish.

On November 15, 2013, the Decision of the Central Committee of the Communist Party of China on Some Major Issues Concerning Comprehensively Deepening Reform passed at the Third Plenary Session of the 18th CPC Central Committee mentioned that while keeping to family planning is a basic state policy, if at least one of a couple is the only child of his or her family, they may have a second child.

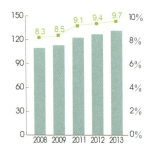

Population Aged 65 Years and Above

■ Senior population (million)
— Percentage in total population

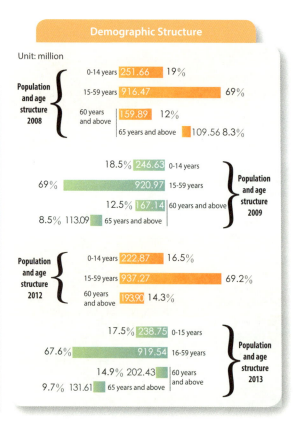

Statistics from the Past Five National Population Censuses

1964

Illiteracy rate
33.58%

Illiterate population 233.27 million

Number of people per million persons having received education of:
Junior college and above 4,160
Senior high /vocational school 13,190
Junior high school 46,800
Elementary school 283,300

1982

Illiteracy rate
22.81%

Illiterate population 229.96 million

Number of people per million persons having received education of:
Junior college and above 6,150
Senior high /vocational school 67,790
Junior high school 178,920
Elementary school 352,370

2010

Illiteracy rate
4.08%

Illiterate population 54.66 million

Number of people per million persons having received education of:
Junior college and above 89,300
Senior high /vocational school 140,320
Junior high school 387,880
Elementary school 267,790

2000

Illiteracy rate
6.72%

Illiterate population 85.07 million

Number of people per million persons having received education of:
Junior college and above 36,110
Senior high /vocational school 111,460
Junior high school 339,610
Elementary school 357,010

1990

Illiteracy rate
15.88%

Illiterate population 180.03 million

Number of people per million persons having received education of:
Junior college and above 14,220
Senior high /vocational school 80,390
Junior high school 233,440
Elementary school 370,570

Note:

1. The starting time of the national population censuses in 1964, 1982 and 1990 was 00:00 on July 1 of their respective years. The starting time of the censuses in 2000 and 2010 was 00:00 on November 1 of their respective years.
2. In all the censuses the total population includes military personnel on active service in the category of urban population.
3. The illiterate population in the 1964 census referred to illiterate persons aged 13 years and above. The illiterate population in the censuses of 1982, 1990, 2000 and 2010 referred to illiterate persons aged 15 years and above.

CHINA

Ethnic Groups

Ethnic Group	Population	Ethnic Group	Population
Han	1.16 billion	De'ang	18,000
Mongolian	5,814,000	Bonan	17,000
Hui	9,817,000	Yugur	14,000
Tibetan	5,416,000	Naxi	309,000
Uygur	8,399,000	Jingpo	132,000
Miao	8,940,000	Va	397,000
Yi	7,762,000	She	710,000
Zhuang	16,179,000	Gaoshan	4,000
Bouyei	2,971,000	Lahu	450,000
Korean	1,924,000	Sui	407,000
Manchu	10,682,000	Gin	23,000
Dong	2,960,000	Tatar	5,000
Yao	2,637,000	Derung	7,000
Bai	1,858,000	Oroqen	8,000
Tujia	8,028,000	Hezhen	5,000
Hani	1,440,000	Monba	9,000
Kazak	1,250,000	Lhoba	2,965
Dai	1,159,000	Jino	21,000
Li	1,248,000	Kirgiz	161,000
Gelao	579,000	Tu	241,000
Xibe	189,000	Daur	132,000
Achang	34,000	Mulam	207,000
Primi	34,000	Qiang	306,000
Tajik	41,000	Blang	92,000
Nu	29,000	Salar	105,000
Uzbek	12,000	Maonan	107,000
Russian	16,000	Lisu	635,000
Ewenki	31,000	Dongxiang	514,000

Statistics from the Fifth National Population Census of 2000

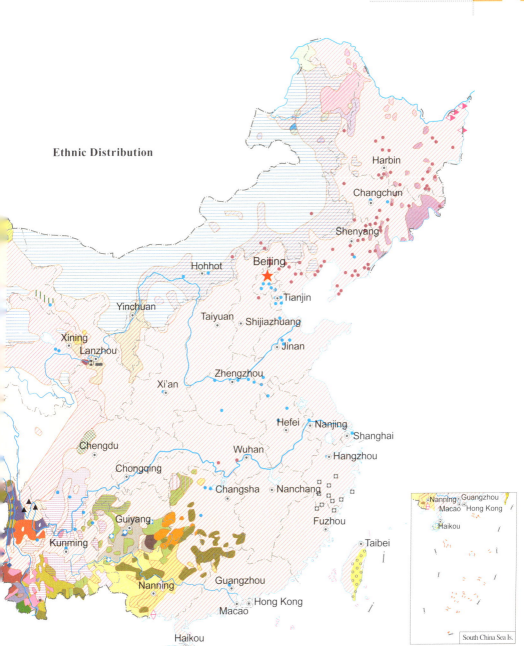

Ethnic Distribution

China is a unitary multi-ethnic country. Fifty-six ethnic groups share this vast land, including the Han, Mongolian, Hui, Tibetan, Manchu and Uygur.

These ethnic groups all vary in costume, diet, tradition and language. The Han people, accounting for more than 90 percent of the total population, are found across the country. The other 55 ethnic groups are called "ethnic minorities." Among the ethnic minorities, the Zhuang have the biggest population – over 16 million – while the population of the Lhoba is the smallest, with only 3,000 or so.

Ethnic Composition

Populations of ethnic groups and their percentages in the populations of the 31 provinces, autonomous regions, municipalities and military personnel on active service on China's mainland:

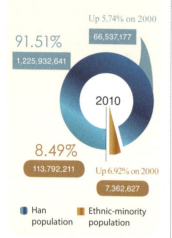

2010

91.51%
1,225,932,641
Up 5.74% on 2000
66,537,177

8.49%
113,792,211
Up 6.92% on 2000
7,362,627

- Han population
- Ethnic-minority population

1 Ethnic minorities deputies at the annual NPC and CPPCC sessions
2 Manchu
3 Traditional Chinese wedding
4 Mongolian
5 Tibetan
6 Uygur

Spoken and Written Languages

Hanyu (standard Chinese language) is the most commonly used language, and *hanzi* (Chinese characters) is the most commonly used written language. All of China's 55 ethnic minorities have their own languages, except for the Hui and the Manchu, who only use Chinese. Nowadays, schools catering mainly to ethnic minority students all use textbooks compiled in their languages and lecture in their languages, while also teaching Chinese and promoting *Hanyu* and standard Chinese characters.

Chinese characters originated from an ideographic system invented by the Chinese people 4,000 years ago, making it the world's oldest ideographic writing system still in use.

Simplified Chinese characters are used on the Chinese mainland and among Chinese communities in Southeast Asia, while traditional Chinese characters are used widely in Hong Kong, Macao, Taiwan Province and among overseas Chinese in North America. In recent years, the use of simplified Chinese characters has grown, as more and more people in other countries are choosing Chinese to study as a second language.

Zhonghua Zihai (*Grand Dictionary of Chinese Characters*), published in 1994, contains more than 85,000 Chinese characters. The official *Xiandai Hanyu Changyong Zibiao* (*List of Frequently Used Characters in Modern Chinese*), promulgated in 1988, contains 2,500 most frequently used characters and 1,000 in less-common use.

Chinese character symbolizing happiness

Chinese character symbolizing longevity

A bean field in Guizhou in which the crops represent the Chinese character meaning "dragon"

Dongba Writing – the Only Living Pictographs

Dongba writing is the ancient pictographic script of the shamans (Dongba) of China's Naxi ethnic group, with a history of over 1,000 years. Originally carved on wood and stone, later it came to be written on paper. There are about 1,400 characters in the script, and they are still in use. It is the only living pictographic language in the world, and is known as a "living fossil," useful for sociological and linguistic research.

Religion

http://www.sara.gov.cn/ is the official website of the State Administration for Religious Affairs, which is affiliated to the State Council.

Taoist priest on Mount Laoshan, Qingdao, Shandong Province

China is a country of great religious diversity, with over 100 million followers of various faiths, including Buddhism, Islam and Christianity (Catholic and Protestant churches), along with China's indigenous Taoism.

Muslims attending a prayer session

China pursues a policy of freedom of religious belief. In China regular religious activities – such as worshiping the Buddha, chanting sutras, praying, expounding on the scriptures, celebrating the Mass, baptism, ordination of monks and nuns, and observance of religious festivals – are all managed by religious personnel and adherents themselves, and protected by law.

Buddhism was introduced to China from India around the first century, and became the most influential religion in China after the fourth century. Tibetan Buddhism, a branch of Chinese Buddhism, is primarily practiced in the Tibet and Inner Mongolia autonomous regions.

Taoism, coming into being in the second century as China's indigenous religion, is based on the philosophy of Lao Zi, who lived in the Spring and Autumn Period (770 BC-476 BC) and his work *Dao De Jing* (*Classic of the Way and Virtue*).

Islam first reached China around the mid-seventh century, and reached its heyday in the Yuan Dynasty (1271-1368). Islam is followed mainly by the Hui, Uyghur and a few other ethnic minorities.

Catholicism was introduced into China in the seventh century, and Protestantism in the early 19th century.

Students of the Serthar Buddhist Institute

Catholic church

http://iwr.cass.cn/ is a network service platform for Buddhism, Christianity, Taoism, Confucianism, Islam, religious theories and arts, and sponsored by the Institute of World Religions of the Chinese Academy of Social Science.

中 国 China

The system of people's congresses defines China's fundamental political system. Multiparty cooperation and political consultation under the leadership of the CPC, regional ethnic autonomy and community-level self-governance constitute China's basic political systems. The state organs include the NPC and its Standing Committee, President of the PRC, State Council, Central Military Commission of the PRC, local people's congresses and local people's governments at various levels, organs of self-government of ethnic autonomous areas, people's courts and people's procuratorates.

Political Systems
and State Structure

- The Constitution
- Socialist System of Laws with Chinese Characteristics
- Political Systems
- National People's Congress
- Presidency
- State Council
- Central Military Commission
- Local People's Congresses and Local People's Governments
- People's Courts
- People's Procuratorates
- Chinese People's Political Consultative Conference
- Political Parties and Other Organizations

The Constitution

Four Amendments to the Constitution

• The 1988 amendment to the Constitution stipulates that the state permits the private sector of the economy to exist and develop within the limits prescribed by law, and the right to the use of land may be transferred in accordance with the law.

• The 1993 amendment stipulates that China practices a socialist market economy, and the system of multiparty cooperation and political consultation under the leadership of the CPC shall continue and develop for a long time to come.

• The 1999 amendment stipulates that the state exercises the rule of law, and upholds the basic economic system in which public ownership is dominant and diverse forms of ownership develop side by side.

• The 2004 amendment stipulates that the lawful private property of citizens is inviolable; the state protects according to law the rights of citizens to private property and to its inheritance; and the state respects and safeguards human rights.

Since the founding of the People's Republic of China (PRC) in 1949, four Constitutions have been formulated successively, in 1954, 1975, 1978 and 1982. The present Constitution contains 138 articles. Amendments to the Constitution have been made four times, the last time being in 2004.

The Constitution stipulates that all citizens are equal before the law and that the state respects and safeguards human rights. It guarantees the basic rights and interests of citizens, including the right to vote and stand for election; freedom of speech, of the press, of assembly, of association, of procession and of demonstration; freedom of religious belief; the inviolability of the freedom of the person, personal dignity, residence and legitimate private property; freedom and privacy of correspondence; the right to criticize and make suggestions regarding any state organ or functionary, and exercise supervision; the right to work and rest, and the right to material assistance from the state and society when old, ill or disabled; and the right to receive education, and freedom to engage in scientific research, literary and artistic creation, and other cultural pursuits.

The Constitution of the People's Republic of China displayed at a bookstore

Socialist System of Laws with Chinese Characteristics

Judges taking oath of office

The overall legislative objective set forth at the 15th CPC National Congress in 1997 was to establish a socialist system of laws with Chinese characteristics by 2010. By the end of 2012 China had formulated 243 general laws, including the Constitution, 721 administrative rules and regulations and 9,200-plus local regulations.

China's legal system, dominated by the Constitution and with Constitution-related laws, civil laws, commercial laws, administrative laws, economic laws, social laws, criminal laws and procedural laws as the main branches, consists of multi-layered laws, administrative rules and regulations, and local regulations governing all economic, political, cultural and social fields.

> http://www.legalinfo.gov.cn/ is the official website of the Ministry of Justice jointly sponsored by the ministry's General Office and Department of Legal Publicity and the newspaper *Legal Daily*. Its purpose is to enhance the people's awareness of law, perfect the rule by law and promote the spirit of socialist rule of law.

Political Systems

Great Hall of the People, Beijing

Besides the implementation of the system of people's congresses as the fundamental political system, the basic structure of China's political system consists of, the system of people's congresses, the system of multiparty cooperation and political consultation under the leadership of the CPC, the system of regional ethnic autonomy and the system of community-level self-governance.

System of People's Congresses

The system of people's congresses is China's fundamental political system. In China, the organs through which the people exercise state power are the National People's Congress (NPC) and local people's congresses. Its basic feature is adherence to the principle of democratic centralism, i.e., the people enjoy extensive democracy and rights, while state power is exercised in a centralized and unified way. On the premise that the people's congresses exercise state power in a unified way, the state's administrative power, judicial authority, procuratorial authority and leadership over the armed forces are clearly separated, so as to ensure that the organs of state power and administrative, judicial and procuratorial and

other state organs work in a coordinated way.

Deputies to the people's congresses at all levels are elected. They include people from all ethnic groups, all walks of life, all regions and all social strata. When the congresses meet they can air their views fully; they can also raise inquiries to governments at the corresponding level and their affiliated departments, and the parties concerned are duty-bound to reply to the inquiries. Electors or constituencies have the right to recall their elected deputies in accordance with the procedures prescribed by law.

System of Multiparty Cooperation and Political Consultation under the Leadership of the CPC

In China the CPC is the ruling party, and rules along with eight participating parties. Before the state adopts important measures or makes decisions on major issues with a bearing on the national economy and the people's well-being, the CPC consults representatives of the eight political parties, as well as people without party affiliation. This system of multiparty cooperation and political consultation under the leadership of the CPC is the basic political system of China.

Multiparty cooperation and political consultation take two principal forms: (1) The Chinese People's Political Consultative Conference (CPPCC); and (2) consultative meetings and forums with the participation of people from non-Communist parties and people without party affiliation, at the invitation of the CPC.

On March 3, 2014, the Second Session of 12th CPPCC National Committee was opened at the Great Hall of the People, Beijing.

Ethnic minorities deputies leaving the Great Hall of the People in Beijing after the Second Session of the 12th NPC on March 13, 2014

The CPPCC National Committee consists of representatives of the CPC, non-Communist parties, people without party affiliation, people's organizations, ethnic minorities and other social strata, and specially invited individuals. The CPPCC National Committee is elected for a term of five years. In addition to attending a plenary session once a year, its members are invited to audit the annual NPC session and fully air their views as non-voting delegates, so as to exercise the functions of political consultation, democratic supervision and participation in the deliberation and administration of state affairs.

Once a year, leaders of the CPC Central Committee invite leaders of the non-Communist parties and representatives of people without party affiliation to consultative meetings, and forums are held every other month. The former focus on major state policies, the latter on exchanges of information, reception of policy proposals and discussion of special issues.

System of Regional Ethnic Autonomy

China practices the system of regional ethnic autonomy. Where ethnic minorities live in compact communities, organs of self-government are established under the unified leadership of the state. As masters in their own areas, the ethnic-minority peoples exercise autonomous power and administer their own internal affairs. The Central Government actively aids the ethnic autonomous areas with funds and materials, so as to promote the development of local economies and cultures.

In addition to the five autonomous regions (Inner Mongolia, Xinjiang Uygur, Guangxi Zhuang, Ningxia Hui and Tibet), China has 30 autonomous prefectures, 120 autonomous counties (banners) and over 1,100 ethnic townships.

The organs of self-government in ethnic autonomous areas are the people's congresses and people's governments of autonomous regions, autonomous prefectures, and autonomous counties (banners). The chairperson or vice-chairs of the standing committee of the local people's congress and the head of an autonomous region, autonomous prefecture or autonomous county (banner) are citizens of the community exercising regional autonomy in the area concerned.

Organs of self-government in ethnic autonomous areas enjoy extensive self-government powers beyond those held by other state organs at the same level. These include: enacting regulations on the exercise of autonomy and separate regulations corresponding to the political, economic and cultural characteristics of the ethnic group(s) in the areas concerned; independently managing and using all revenues accruing to the ethnic autonomous areas; independently arranging and managing local economic development, education, science, culture, public health and physical culture, protecting their cultural heritage, and developing their cultures.

Consultative Democracy

The Decision of the Central Committee of the Communist Party of China on Some Major Issues Concerning Comprehensively Deepening the Reform, adopted on November 15, 2013, called for promoting consultative democracy in an extensive, multilevel and systematic way.

Consultative democracy is a particular form and a unique advantage of China's socialist democracy. Under the leadership of the CPC, extensive consultancy is conducted throughout society on major issues concerning economic and social development and practical problems regarding the people's interests, and resolute consultation is made before decision-making and during the implementation of decisions.

The Decision recommended the building of a consultative democracy with appropriate and complete procedures, and the expansion of consultation channels covering organs of state power, CPPCC committees, political parties, community-level and social organizations. Consultation will be made in terms of legislation, administration, democracy, government affairs and social issues, new think tanks with Chinese characteristics will be promoted, and a sound consultancy system for decision-making will be built.

Villagers of Wanfu in Zhejiang Province witnessing the recording of ballots for electing their village chief, December 23, 2013

System of Community-level Self-governance

China's community-level self-governance refers to the system in which urban and rural residents, in accordance with relevant laws and policies, directly conduct democratic elections, make decisions, engage in discussions and exercise democratic supervision through community-level self-governance organs under the leadership of community-level CPC organizations in their residential areas. Community-level self-governance could guarantee people self-management, self-service, self-education and self-supervision. This is the most effective and widely applied way for the people to be their own masters.

Through the residents' or villagers' committees established among urban and rural residents on the basis of their place of residence, and through workers' congresses of each enterprise and public institution, residents, villagers and workers manage public affairs and social services in their areas or workplaces, mediate civil disputes, help maintain public order, convey residents' or workers' opinions and demands, and make suggestions to the people's government.

National People's Congress

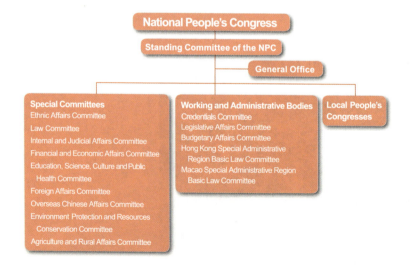

On March 5, 2014, the Second Session of the 12th NPC was opened at the Great Hall of the People, Beijing.

The NPC, the highest organ of state power, is composed of deputies elected from all provinces, autonomous regions, municipalities directly under the Central Government, special administrative regions and the armed forces. It exercises legislative power and makes decisions on major issues regarding national political life. Its main functions and powers: to enact and amend laws; to examine and approve the plan for national economic and social development, and the state budget, and the reports on their implementation; to make decisions on questions of war and peace; to elect or decide on the leadership of the highest organs of state, i.e. Chairman of the Standing Committee of the NPC, President of the PRC, Premier of the State Council and Chairman of the Central Military Commission, with the power to remove from office any of the above persons.

The NPC is elected for a term of five years, and is now in its 12th term. The current Chairman of the NPC Standing Committee is **Zhang Dejiang**.

Presidency

The President of the PRC and the Standing Committee of the NPC jointly exercise the functions and powers of the head of state. The President, pursuant to decisions of the NPC and its Standing Committee, promulgates laws; appoints or removes members of the State Council; confers state medals and titles of honor; promulgates amnesty decrees; declares national emergencies, wars and mobilizations; and on behalf of the PRC, conducts state activities; receives foreign diplomatic representatives; appoints or recalls plenipotentiary representatives abroad; and ratifies or abrogates treaties and important agreements reached with foreign states. The current President of the PRC is **Xi Jinping.**

State Council

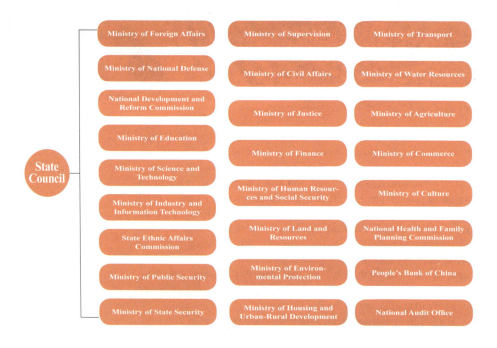

The State Council is the Central People's Government. It is the executive body of the highest organ of state power, and the highest organ of state administration. The State Council is responsible to the NPC and its Standing Committee, and reports to them on its work. The State Council has the power to adopt administrative measures, enact administrative regulations, and promulgate decisions and orders within its functions and powers. The State Council is composed of the Premier, Vice Premiers, State Councilors, Secretary-general, Ministers in charge of ministries or commissions, Governor of the People's Bank of China, and Auditor-general of the National Audit Office. The current Premier of the State Council is **Li Keqiang**.

> http://www.gov.cn is a comprehensive platform on which the State Council and its departments, and people's governments of provinces, autonomous regions and municipalities directly under the Central Government release government information and provide online services.

Central Military Commission

The Central Military Commission is the nation's leading organ and commander of the armed forces. China's armed forces consist of the Chinese People's Liberation Army (PLA), the Chinese People's Armed Police Force, and the Militia. The PLA is the standing army of the state. The main tasks of the Armed Police Force include performing guard duties and maintaining public order, as empowered by the state. The Militia is an armed force of the masses and, when not on duty, remains engaged in normal production activities. The Central Military Commission is composed of the Chair, Vice Chairs and other members. The current Chairman is **Xi Jinping**.

China pursues a national defense policy which is defensive in nature. In accordance with the Constitution and other relevant laws, the armed forces undertake the sacred duty of resisting foreign aggression, defending the motherland, and safeguarding overall social stability and peace for the people. To build a fortified national defense and strong armed forces compatible with national security and development interests is a strategic task of China's modernization, and a common cause of the people of all ethnic groups. The goals and tasks of China's national defense in the new era: to safeguard national sovereignty, security and development interests; maintain social harmony and stability; accelerate the modernization of national defense and the armed forces; and contribute to world peace and stability.

Frontier guards watching the territorial seas

Local People's Congresses and Local People's Governments

Reflecting China's existing national administrative divisions, there are people's congresses and people's governments at all levels – in provinces, autonomous regions and municipalities directly under the Central Government; in counties and cities; and in townships and towns.

The people's congresses at and above the county level have standing committees. The local people's congresses are the local organs of state power. They have the power to decide on important affairs in their respective administrative areas. The people's congresses of provinces, autonomous regions and municipalities directly under the Central Government have the power to formulate local regulations.

Local people's governments are the local administrative organs. Working under the unified leadership of the State Council, they are responsible and report on their work to the people's congresses and their standing committees at the corresponding level and to the organs of state administration at the next higher level. They have overall responsibility for the administrative work within their respective administrative areas.

People's Courts

The people's courts are the judicial organs of the state. The Supreme People's Court is established at the state level; higher people's courts are established in provinces, autonomous regions and municipalities directly under the Central Government; and intermediate and primary people's courts at lower levels.

The Supreme People's Court, the state's highest judicial organ, reports to the NPC and its Standing Committee, and supervises the judicial work of the local people's courts at various levels, the military courts and other special people's courts. The current President of the Supreme People's Court is **Zhou Qiang**.

Sacred gavel used in courts of law

People's Procuratorates

The people's procuratorates are the organs of legal supervision of the state. Their organization corresponds to that of the people's courts. The people's procuratorates complete tasks through exercising procuratorial power. They exercise this authority over cases endangering state and public security, damaging economic order and infringing on citizens' personal and democratic rights, as well as over other important criminal cases; examine cases scheduled for investigation by public security agencies, and decide on whether suspects should be arrested or not, and whether cases should be prosecuted or exempted from prosecution; institute and support public prosecutions in criminal cases; and oversee the activities of public security agencies, people's courts, prisons, houses of detention and reform-through-labor institutions. The current Procurator-general of the Supreme People's Procuratorate is **Cao Jianming**.

Chinese People's Political Consultative Conference

> **The NPC, the CPPCC and the State Council**
>
> The NPC exercises power through election, ballot and voting. The CPPCC is fully consulted before elections and balloting. The NPC and the CPPCC exist as the two most important forms of China's socialist democracy. The CPPCC is consulted before policy-making, after which the NPC votes on policy-making, and the State Council is responsible for policy implementation. They assume separate duties, with full cooperation and mutual reliance, while complementing each other under the unified leadership of the CPC. This political system with Chinese characteristics is suited to China's actual conditions.

The CPPCC is an organization of the Chinese people's patriotic united front as well as an important institution of multi-party cooperation and political consultation under the leadership of the CPC. It is an important channel for promoting socialist democracy in China. The main functions of the CPPCC: political consultation, democratic supervision, and participation in the deliberation and administration of state affairs. The CPPCC has its National Committee and local committees.

CPPCC National Committee

The CPPCC National Committee consists of members of the CPC and non-Communist parties, people without party affiliation, representatives of people's organizations, ethnic minorities and people of all walks of life, representatives of the Hong Kong and Macao special administrative regions, Taiwan Province and returned overseas Chinese, and specially invited individuals. The CPPCC National Committee is elected for a term of five years, and is now in its 12th term. The 12th CPPCC National Committee held its first session in Beijing March 3 to 12, 2013 to elect its new leaders. The current Chairman of the CPPCC National Committee is **Yu Zhengsheng**.

CPPCC Local Committees

CPPCC committees have been set up in all provinces, autonomous regions, municipalities directly under the Central Government; autonomous prefectures and cities divided into districts; counties, autonomous counties, cities not divided into districts and districts under the jurisdiction of cities.

Political Parties and Other Organizations

Communist Party of China

The Communist Party of China (CPC) was established in 1921. It immediately led the Chinese people to carry out painstaking struggles, winning the New-democratic Revolution and founding the People's Republic of China in 1949. After New China was founded, the CPC guided the Chinese people to set up the fundamental system of socialism, begin massive socialist construction, secure China's political base and lay the material and institutional foundations for China's development and progress. Since 1978 the CPC has

Venue of the CPC's First National Congress in Shanghai

 New Organs

In 2013 the Third Plenary Session of the 18th CPC Central Committee made the decision to set up several new organs, including a leading group for comprehensively deepening the reform, the Council of State Security, a department responsible for the control of territorial utilization, and the system of the leadership for Internet management.

The Leading Group for Deepening the Reform Comprehensively, headed by Xi Jinping, was set up to take charge of making an overall reform plan, coordinating reform in different sectors, advancing reform endeavors as a whole and supervising the implementation of the reform plan. The Council of State Security, chaired by Xi Jinping, is a coordinating organ of the CPC Central Committee responsible for relevant decision-making and consultancy. It was set up to coordinate important issues and work regarding state security.

directed the Chinese people to implement the reform and opening up policies, and initiate and develop socialism with Chinese characteristics, promoting China's modern march into a new era.

By the end of 2013 the number of CPC members had reached 85.127 million. The highest leading organ of the CPC is the National Congress, which is held once every five years. When the National Congress is not in session, the Central Committee implements its decisions and leads all the work of the Party. The current General Secretary of the CPC Central Committee is **Xi Jinping**.

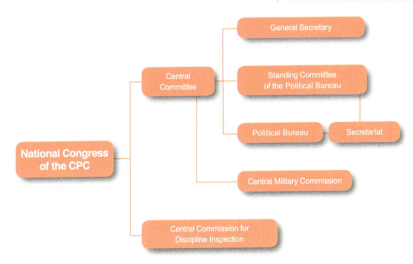

Non-communist Parties

Besides the CPC, China has eight other political parties. These parties all support the CPC's political leadership, while enjoying political freedom, organizational independence and lawful equality within the scope of the Constitution. The basic principle of cooperation between the CPC and these parties is long-term coexistence, mutual supervision, treating each other with sincerity and sharing each other's weal and woe.

Many of the members of these parties hold posts on the standing committees of the people's congresses, CPPCC committees, government organs, or economic, cultural, educational, scientific and technological departments. For instance, the chairpersons of the eight parties' central committees are currently vice-chairs of the NPC Standing Committee or the CPPCC National Committee. With a combined membership exceeding 700,000, they have set up branches and community-level organizations in all provinces, autonomous regions and municipalities directly under the Central Government, and in large and medium-sized cities.

The Eight Non-communist Parties

Revolutionary Committee of the Chinese Kuomintang
- Main constituents: Former Kuomintang members and people having historical connections with the Kuomintang
- Date of founding: January 1948
- Chairman of the central committee: Wan Exiang

China Association for the Promotion of Democracy
- Main Constituents: Higher and mid-level intellectuals working in educational, cultural, scientific, publishing and other fields
- Date of Founding: December 1945
- Chairwoman of the central committee: Yan Junqi

China Democratic League
- Main constituents: Higher and mid-level intellectuals specializing in culture, education, and science and technology
- Date of founding: October 1941
- Chairman of the central committee: Zhang Baowen

Chinese Peasants and Workers Democratic Party
- Main constituents: Higher and mid-level intellectuals in medical, cultural, educational and sci-tech fields
- Date of founding: August 1930
- Chairman of the central committee: Chen Zhu

China Democratic National Construction Association
- Main constituents: Specialists and scholars in the economic field
- Date of founding: December 1945
- Chairman of the central committee: Chen Changzhi

China Zhi Gong Dang
- Main constituents: Returned overseas Chinese, relatives of overseas Chinese, and representative individuals and specialists and scholars with overseas connections
- Date of foundation: October 1925
- Chairman of the central committee: Wan Gang

Jiu San Society
- Main constituents: Higher and mid-level intellectuals specializing in science and technology, culture, education and medicine
- Date of founding: December 1944
- Chairman of the central committee: Han Qide

Taiwan Democratic Self-government League
- Main constituents: People born or with family roots in Taiwan Province and currently residing on the mainland
- Date of founding: November 1947
- Chairwoman of the central committee: Lin Wenyi

Main Mass Organizations

All-China Federation of Trade Unions
Established: 1925
Chairman: Li Jianguo

Communist Youth League of China
Established: 1922
First Secretary: Qin Yizhi

All-China Women's Federation
Established: 1949
Chairwoman: Shen Yueyue

China Association for Science and Technology
Established: 1958
President: Han Qide

All-China Federation of Returned Overseas Chinese
Established: 1956
Chairman: Lin Jun

All-China Federation of Taiwan Compatriots
Established: 1981
Chairman: Liang Guoyang

All-China Youth Federation
Established: 1949
Chairman: Wang Xiao

All-China Federation of Industry and Commerce
Established: 1953
Chairman: Wang Qinmin

Chinese People's Association for Friendship with Foreign Countries
Established: 1954
Chairwoman: Li Xiaolin

Mass Organizations and NGOs

Chinese mass organizations carry out their activities independently and in accordance with the Constitution and the law. Their branches cover both urban and rural areas. They participate in national and local political life, and play an important role in coordinating social and public affairs, and safeguarding the legitimate rights and interests of the people.

Chinese NGOs are mainly engaged in technology, education, culture, health, sports, environmental protection, legal services, and intermediary services. Environmental NGOs have become an important force for spreading environmental education and promoting public participation in environmental protection.

> http://cpc.people.com.cn/ is an authoritative website introducing the CPC in a systematic and comprehensive way, releasing news of important activities and speeches of leading officials of the CPC Central Committee, elaborating on important meetings and documents, and giving briefings on all the work of the Party. It has also opened several interactive columns to enhance exchanges between Party members and the Party, between Party members themselves, and between Party members and the masses.

中　国　C h i n a

Upholding the principles of peace, development, cooperation, mutual benefit, and adhering to the concept of putting people's interests first and conducting diplomacy for the people, China firmly safeguards its national sovereignty, security and development interests, and makes every effort to protect the legitimate rights and interests of Chinese nationals and legal persons overseas. China advocates mutually beneficial cooperation as the fundamental solution to maintaining sound and stable development of international relations in the new era. All countries and peoples should enjoy the fruits of development and every country should promote common progress together with other countries while seeking self-development.

Within the present world setup, China pursues an opening strategy of mutual benefit, develops all-round friendship and cooperation with other countries on the basis of the Five Principles of Peaceful Co-existence, and undertakes its responsibilities in the building of a world of lasting peace and common prosperity.

Foreign Relations

- Foreign Policy
- Friendship with Neighboring Countries
- Cooperation with Other Developing Countries
- Cooperation with Major Countries
- Multilateral Diplomacy

Foreign Policy

http://www.fmprc.gov.cn/

The Ministry of Foreign Affairs is the department under the State Council which is responsible for handling diplomatic affairs between the Chinese government and the governments of other countries or inter-governmental organizations.

China's foreign policy aims to uphold world peace and promote common development. China pursues an independent foreign policy of peace, follows the path of peaceful development, adheres to an opening strategy of mutual benefit and win-win results, and endeavors to build a harmonious world of lasting peace and common prosperity. It is committed to developing friendship and cooperation with all other countries on the basis of the Five Principles of Peaceful Coexistence.

China is committed to enhancing friendly relations with its neighbors, and actively participates in developing cooperative mechanisms, so as to expand regional cooperation, and create a regional environment of peace and stability, equality and mutual trust, cooperation and mutual benefit. It will enhance links with other developing countries, deepen traditional friendships, expand mutually beneficial cooperation, help achieve the UN Millennium Development Goals, and uphold the legitimate rights and interests as well as the common interests of developing countries. It will increase strategic dialogue with developed countries to enhance strategic mutual trust,

Chinese folk arts like paper cutting are popular in many countries and regions.

expand cooperation, and promote long-term, steady and sound growth in China's relations with these countries. It actively engages in multilateral issues and global governance, and work to make the international order fairer and more equitable.

The Chinese people will make unremitting efforts together with other peoples to uphold world peace and promote common development and prosperity for all.

China had established diplomatic relations with 172 countries as of May 2013.

Friendship with Neighboring Countries

As the country with the largest number of neighboring states, China follows the policy of friendship and partnership with its neighbors and persists in creating an amicable, secure and prosperous neighborhood, which highlights amity, sincerity, mutual benefit and inclusiveness. China promotes, safeguards and cherishes the peace and stability of the surrounding environment.

In recent years, it has conducted cooperation with its neighbors on the basis of mutual benefit. It exerts itself to promote more common interests with them and raise cooperation with them to higher levels, so as to make other countries enjoy the benefits of China's growth while China obtains advantages from common development. At the same time, China firmly defends its territorial sovereignty on land and sea, and endeavors to settle territorial and jurisdictional disputes with its neighbors and peacefully resolve issues carried over from history through negotiations with the relevant countries.

China works to strengthen mutually beneficial cooperation with neighboring countries, and improve the current regional and sub-regional cooperative mechanisms of the China-ASEAN Free Trade Area, 10+3 (10 member countries of the ASEAN and China, Japan and the Republic of Korea), 10+1 (ASEAN and China), East Asia Summit (ESA) and the Greater Mekong Sub-region cooperation. It endeavors to promote regional economic integration such as the China-ASEAN Free

Conference on Interaction and Confidence Building Measures in Asia (CICA)

CICA is an inter-governmental forum for enhancing cooperation and confidence in the endeavor to promote peace, security and stability in Asia. With 26 member states and 12 observer states and organizations from all regions of Asia with their different social systems, and representing various religions, cultures and developmental stages, CICA is a comprehensive organization.

The Fourth CICA Summit, presided over by Chinese President Xi Jinping, was held in the Shanghai Expo Center in May 2014. At the summit, China formally took over the CICA chairmanship for the period 2014-2016. Leaders and representatives of all participating states and organizations thought highly of the Summit, and supported Xi's concept for Asia's security and proposal to create the Silk Road Economic Belt and the 21st Century Maritime Silk Road, which, they believe, can enhance cooperation, promote economic recovery and development, and finally achieve the lofty goal pursued by the whole of Asia.

At the Western Pacific Naval Symposium sponsored by Chinese Navy on April 22, 2014 in Qingdao, the Indonesian navy band attracted a big audience.

Trade Area, is open-minded to other proposals for regional cooperation, and welcomes any initiatives by countries outside the region to play a constructive role in promoting regional peace and development.

Chinese President Xi Jinping has visited Russia, Central Asian countries, Indonesia, Malaysia, the Republic of Korea, Mongolia, India and other countries since assuming the presidency of China in March 2013, while Premier Li Keqiang has visited India, Pakistan, Brunei, Thailand and Vietnam since he took over the premiership, demonstrating China's emphasis on relations with neighboring countries.

Cooperation with Other Developing Countries

Elementary education officials from 26 African countries visited several primary schools of Jiangxi Province in April 2014.

As a developing country, China has adopted as a cornerstone of its foreign policy a strategy of strengthening solidarity and cooperation with other developing countries and better safeguarding the common interests of developing countries.

China firmly upholds a friendly policy toward African countries, and makes unremitting efforts to maintain peace and stability in Africa. Through the Forum on China and Africa Cooperation (FOCAC) and other channels, China contributes to Africa's prosperity and development. In March 2013 Chinese President Xi Jinping paid state visits to Tanzania, South Africa and the Republic of Congo as stops on his first foreign trip after assuming the presidency, and invited 14 senior African guests for a breakfast meeting. He said China will unswervingly pursue a friendly policy toward Africa no matter what changes take place in the international situation. China will continue to be a reliable friend and sincere partner of African countries, continuing to contribute to their peace and development.

The establishment of a China-Arab strategic cooperative relationship featuring all-round cooperation and common progress is in keeping with the common aspirations of both sides. The two sides endeavor to build strategic China-Arab relations within the China-Arab States Cooperation Forum (CASCF) framework by expanding exchanges at various lev-

Exhibition of Latin American photographers at Wuhan Museum, Hubei Province in autumn 2013

els, strengthening cooperation in various fields, and encouraging dialogue between different civilizations.

China is committed to establishing and developing comprehensive partnership with Latin America and the Caribbean countries based on equality, mutual benefit and common progress. With the China-CELAC Forum as the core, an overall cooperative mechanism between China and Latin America and the Caribbean countries has been established. Since China became a major trading partner of Latin America, the two sides have constantly refined their trade structure, and achieved mutually beneficial development that is complementary and sustainable. China continues to support the equal participation of Pacific islands countries in international affairs, and to promote their economic and social development. During his state visits in Trinidad and Tobago, Costa Rica and Mexico in May 2013, Chinese President Xi Jinping held bilateral dialogues with leaders of eight Caribbean countries, significantly deepening overall China-CELAC cooperation.

Forum on China-Africa Cooperation (FOCAC)

FOCAC is a collective dialogue mechanism within the framework of South-South cooperation between China and African countries. In the 1990s peace and development gradually became the trend of the times. The international community, particularly developing countries, moved to build a new international political and economic order in a multi-polar world. As suggested by some African countries, China proposed to hold the first ministerial conference of FOCAC in Beijing in 2000, and received active responses and support from African countries. The ministerial conference of FOCAC is held every three years, and a senior official preparatory meeting is held a year before the ministerial conference.

Cooperation with Major Countries

Sino-US Relations

In recent years China and the United States have maintained high-level strategic communications, and established mechanisms for strategic and economic dialogues, and high-level consultations on people-to-people exchanges. On June 7 and 8, 2013, Chinese President Xi Jinping held the first meetings of his presidency with US President Barack Obama at the Annenberg Estate in California. The two leaders exchanged in-depth views on a wide range of major strategic issues of common concern, including Sino-US relations, economic and military cooperation, and how to tackle regional and global challenges, with the aim of improving mutual understanding, strategic mutual trust and practical cooperation between the two sides. Their meeting put forward guidelines for jointly building a new model of major-country relationship between China and the US that can be summarized as "no conflict, no confrontation, mutual respect and win-win cooperation."

In spite of the differences in political systems, values, historical and cultural traditions and development levels of economy and society between the two sides, China and the US continue to deepen their high-level contacts, promote trade, investment, people-to-people exchanges and local cooperation, enhance mutual military trust, and keep close and effective communication and coordination on major regional and global issues. US First Lady Michelle Obama and her family visited China March 20-26, 2014. In the same month Xi and Obama met at the Hague, agreeing to work together to improve the new model of relationship between the two countries.

Sino-Russian Relations

Since the Treaty on Good-neighborliness, Friendship and Cooperation Between China and Russia was signed in 2001, China and Russia have become each other's most important strategic partner, forming a comprehensive strategic partnership.

Facing the complex international situation and fragile

global economic environment, both countries are increasing mutual political support, firmly backing the other's efforts to safeguard national sovereignty, security and development interests, unswervingly defending the other to take a path in line with its own national conditions and steadfastly standing by the other's development and rejuvenation. The two countries are also expanding their practical cooperation, transforming their favorable political relations into actual results and achieving common development.

Moreover, both sides are closely coordinating in international and regional affairs, improving their common strategic security, safeguarding the principles of the UN Charter and basic norms of international relations, upholding the results of World War II and international order ever since, protecting international fairness and justice, and helping to bring about a peaceful, stable and prosperous world.

In March 2013 Chinese President Xi Jinping paid the first state visit of his presidency to Russia. In September and October of the same year, Xi met Russian President Vladimir Putin in Russia's St. Petersburg and on Indonesia's Bali Island. In February 2014 Xi met Putin in Russia again when he attended the opening ceremony of the Sochi Winter Olympic Games, which was also the first time for a Chinese president to attend an international sports event in a foreign country. Chinese Premier Li Keqiang also frequently met his Russian counterpart Dmitry Medvedev through visits, regular meetings and international or regional conferences.

Chinese and Russian navies conducted a live combat drill – "Joint Sea–2014" – on the East China Sea, May 24, 2014.

Sino-EU Relations

China established formal diplomatic relations with the European Economic Community in 1975, and a comprehensive strategic partnership with the European Union (EU) in 2003. By the end of 2013 the two sides had conducted 16 meetings between various leaders and held four high-level strategic dialogues, and set up various mechanisms for dialogue and cooperation at different levels pertaining to politics, economy and trade, science and technology, and energy and the environment. The EU was China's largest trading partner, while China was the EU's second-largest by the end of 2013.

Chinese President Xi Jinping visited the Netherlands, France, Germany and Belgium as well as the EU headquarters

A math contest was held to mark the 50th anniversary of Sino-French diplomatic relations in 2014.

in Brussels, Belgium, from March 22 to April 2, 2014. During his meetings with leaders of various countries, he proposed to build four partnerships featuring peace, growth, reform and progress of civilization to bridge the two major forces, two major markets and two major civilizations of China and the EU.

Sino-Japanese Relations

China and Japan are close neighbors facing each other across a narrow strip of water. As two weighty countries in Asia and the world, China and Japan bear the responsibility to maintain the peace, stability and prosperity of the region and the world. A stable friendly relationship in the long run acts in the fundamental interests of both countries and peoples, as well as the peace, stability and prosperity of the region and the world.

Japan holds erroneous views on historical and territorial issues, which poses the main obstacle to the path of Sino-Japanese relations. It is vital for the development of Sino-Japanese relations to properly handle the issues left over by history. China hopes that Japan can draw a lesson from history and work together with China to safeguard historic justice and develop relations for the future on the basis of the four political documents between China and Japan.

Multilateral Diplomacy

With increasing involvement in the international community, the range and depth of China's participation in multilateral diplomacy has significantly increased. China is now an active participant in and advocate of the mechanism and actions of multilateral diplomacy. Chinese leaders regularly attend the UN assemblies, Asia-Pacific Economic Cooperation (APEC) meetings, and Asia-Europe Meeting (ASEM), G20 and BRICS summits, playing an active role in promoting international and regional cooperation, and improving the country's image and status globally.

China actively carries out regional multilateral diplomacy within the framework of regional organizations and regional multilateral mechanisms. In the fields of politics and security, China has successfully organized many rounds of six-party talks on the Korean Peninsula nuclear issue, taken an active part in the Association of Southeast Asian Nations (ASEAN) Regional Forum, and promoted cooperation between the Shanghai Cooperation Organization (SCO) member states. In the field of economic development, it has taken practical measures to promote regional economic cooperation and integration, not only playing an important role in APEC, but also accelerating the construction of the China-ASEAN Free Trade Area.

China encourages South-North dialogue, inter-continental cooperation and cooperation with special organizations.

Boao Forum for Asia (BFA)

Against the backdrop of quickened globalization and increased regional cooperation of Asia, the BFA was formally inaugurated in Boao, a small town in China's Hainan Province, in late February 2001 by 25 Asian countries and Australia. It is a non-governmental and non-profit international organization with a fixed conference date and a fixed domicile, serving as a high-end platform for dialogues among leaders of national governments, industrial and business circles, and academic circles of countries in Asia and other continents about the important issues concerning the economy, society and environment in Asia, and the world as a whole. Boao is the permanent site of the BFA Headquarters. The BFA Annual Conference 2014, with the theme "Asia's New Future: Identifying New Growth Drivers," was held April 8-11, 2014.

Meeting site of the Boao Forum for Asia

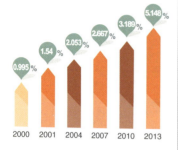

China's Assessed Financial Contributions to the UN

0.995% 1.54% 2.053% 2.667% 3.189% 5.148%
2000 2001 2004 2007 2010 2013

Through the platforms of ASEM, FOCAC, CASCF, Davos summit, BFA and special industry conferences, it plays an active and responsible role in the cause of preserving a just and reasonable new international order, resolving financial crises, and coping with global warming. China also plays a constructive role in addressing the situation on the Korean Peninsula, the Iranian nuclear issue, the Middle East issue, the issue of Ukraine and other regional hot-spots.

China and the UN

As a permanent member of the UN Security Council, China is a solid supporter and major partner of the UN. It supports and practices multilateralism, and is committed to safeguarding the primary purposes and principles of the UN Charter and the UN's position of authority. China advocates peaceful solutions to international disputes through dialogue and negotiation. It believes that the UN, as the core of multilateral organizations and mechanisms, plays an irreplaceable role in safeguarding world peace, and promoting common progress and international cooperation.

China consistently supports and actively participates in UN peacekeeping missions. Its peacekeepers constitute one of the biggest contingents from among all the Security Council's permanent members. Chinese President Xi Jinping visited the UNESCO headquarters in March 2014 and delivered a speech, stating China's opinions on exchanges and mutual learning among civilizations, and calling for different civilizations to respect each other and live in harmony.

UN Security Council holding an open meeting on the Ukraine situation, New York, March 19, 2014 (local time)

APEC SME Summit, Shenzhen, Guangdong Province, December 19, 2013

China and APEC

Established in 1989, APEC is the highest and most influential economic cooperative mechanism in the Asia-Pacific region, and the largest conglomerate organization for the multilateral regional economy. China highly values the role played by APEC. Chinese leaders have attended all 21 APEC Economic Leaders' Meetings since 1993. China always supports and takes an active part in cooperation with APEC at various levels and in various fields, making significant contributions to the continuous progress of such cooperation. China hosted the 9th APEC Economic Leaders' Meeting in Shanghai in 2001, and will host the 22nd Meeting in Beijing in 2014.

http://www.apec-china.org.cn/
Website of the organizing committee of 2014 APEC Meeting in Beijing.

China and the SCO

On April 26, 1996 the heads of state of China, Russia, Kazakhstan, Kyrgyzstan and Tajikistan formally created the Shanghai Five mechanism when meeting in Shanghai for the first time, and the SCO was established on the basis of that mechanism on June 15, 2001. It was the first international organization established in China and named after a Chinese city. By the end of 2013 the SCO had six member states and five observers.

China has constantly facilitated the good-neighborly friendship and cooperation between the SCO member states, and promoted the Organization's substantive cooperation and mechanism-building process. On September 13, 2013 Chinese

President Xi Jinping and heads of other states at the 13th SCO Council of Heads of States, Kyrgyzstan, September 13, 2013

> http://www.sectsco.org/
> The official website of the SCO, introducing the SCO, member states, documents and others.

President Xi Jinping attended on invitation the 13th Meeting of the Council of Heads of the Member States of the SCO in Bishkek, Kyrgyzstan, and delivered an important speech titled "Carrying Forward the 'Shanghai Spirit' and Promoting Common Development." On November 29, 2013 Chinese Premier Li Keqiang attended the 12th prime ministers' meeting of the SCO member states in Uzbekistan.

China and BRICS

BRICS was originally known as BRIC, an acronym for an association of the four major emerging economies of Brazil, Russia, India and China before it admitted South Africa to full membership in December 2010.

In March 2013, during the 5th BRICS Summit in Durban, South Africa, Chinese President Xi Jinping delivered a speech titled "Working Together for Common Development." Xi said that China would keep strengthening cooperation with the other BRICS countries in order to boost the growth of member countries, and improve their cooperation framework to bring about more positive results, thus benefiting people of all countries and making a further contribution to world peace and development.

China and ASEAN

In recent years, high-level officials of ASEAN and China have exchanged frequent visits, which facilitated the rapid development of cooperation in the fields of politics, economy, trade, science and technology, and culture.

The China-ASEAN (10+1) Summit is a regular leaders' meeting between the 10 ASEAN member countries (Brunei, Indonesia, Malaysia, the Philippines, Singapore, Thailand, Vietnam, Laos, Myanmar and Cambodia) and China.

In the process of globalization in the late 1990s the ASEAN countries gradually realized the importance of creating new-level and all-round relations with the outside world, and determined to carry out economic cooperation with other countries. The China-ASEAN cooperative mechanism was founded in such an environment. Later, the mechanism was extended to the political, security and cultural spheres while focusing on economic cooperation, forming a multi-level,

Demonstration of Zhuang embroidery technique during China-ASEAN Expo in Nanning, Guangxi, May 31, 2014

wide-ranging and comprehensive cooperation pattern. Within its framework, summits, ministerial meetings, high-level officials' meetings and working group meetings are held on an annual basis.

In October 2013 Chinese Premier Li Keqiang attended the 16th China-ASEAN (10+1) Summit in Brunei. At the Summit, the leaders held in-depth discussions on deepening China-ASEAN relations, raised proposals for further cooperation and reached broad consensus.

China and the G20

The Group of Twenty Finance Ministers and Central Bank Governors, commonly known as the G20, is an international economic cooperation forum that was formally inaugurated at the G8 Finance Ministers' Meeting in Washington on September 25, 1999. As an informal dialogue mechanism within the framework of the Bretton Woods System, and comprising the former G8 countries and 12 other important economies, it focuses on bringing together important industrialized and emerging economies to open-mindedly and constructively discuss and study key substantive issues, so as to seek cooperation in the course of promoting global financial stability and sustainable economic growth.

A member since its inception, China has attended all G20 ministerial and deputies meetings. China held the chair of the G20 in 2005, hosting the 7th Finance Ministers and Central Bank Governors Meeting and two deputies meetings, as well as relevant seminars.

Chinese President Xi Jinping attended the 8th G20 Leaders' Summit in September 2013 in St. Petersburg, Russia, and made an important speech. He stressed that, with a broad vision for the future, all countries should make efforts to create a global economy, in which their innovations are facilitated, their economic growth patterns interact and their interests are integrated. He advocated that all countries maintain and develop an open world economy, build a closer economic partnership, and undertake their due responsibilities. He said that China would deepen its reform and adhere to the opening strategy of mutual benefit. China, he affirmed, has the conditions and ability to achieve sustainable and sound economic development.

G20 Summit, St. Petersburg, Russia, September 6, 2013 (local time)

中　国　C h i n a

After more than 30 years of reform and opening up, a socialist market economy has been basically established in China, and an omni-directional pattern of opening up which is wide-ranging and multi-level with priorities has taken shape. China's economy has thus made great strides.

Currently, with the overall goal of comprehensively deepening reform, China is deepening its economic structural reform by centering on letting the market play the decisive role, upholding and improving the basic economic system, accelerating the perfection of a modern market system, macro-control system and open economy system, transforming economic development pattern, and building an innovative country to make the economic growth more efficient, fair and sustainable.

Economy

- Economic Development and Transformation
- Economic Structural Reform
- Economic Restructuring
- Innovation-driven Development
- All-round Opening Up
- Coordinated Development of All Regions
- Agriculture
- Industry
- Service Industry

Economic Development and Transformation

Sewage treatment plant

http://www.ce.cn/
Boasting over 40 categorized databases on economics in Chinese, English and German versions, www.ce.cn aims to provide information mainly on economic reporting, everyday news and economic services, and offers contents covering social and political events, industrial market, real estate market, and the international and regional economies.

Taking economic development as the central task is vital to national renewal. China's economic development is guided by its "Five-year Plans." Now the country is undertaking its 12th Five-year Plan (2011-2015). Currently, its GDP has reached No. 2 in the world thanks to its sustained and rapid development since the launch of the reform and opening up program some three decades ago.

China's huge population and relatively backward state of development determines that it is potentially one of the biggest and most promising economies in the world though still one of the developing countries.

Currently, with the overall goal of comprehensively deepening reform, China is taking the pursuit of development in a scientific way as the underlying guideline, and accelerating the change of its growth model as a major task to ensure the development is based on improved quality and performance. It inspires all type of market participants with new vigor for development, increase motivation for pursuing innovation-driven development, and establish a new system for developing modern industries. It works to create new and favorable conditions for developing the open economy. This will make economic development become driven more by domestic demand, especially consumer demand, by a modern service industry and strategic emerging industries, by scientific and technological progress, by a workforce of higher quality and innovation in management, by resource conservation and a circular economy, and by coordinated and mutually reinforcing urban-rural development and development between regions. Taking these steps will enable China to sustain long-term development.

Fixed Assets Investment in 2013

West: 10.9228 trillion yuan
up 22.8% over 2012

East: 17.9092 trillion yuan
up 17.9% over 2012

Central: 10.5894 trillion yuan
up 22.2% over 2012

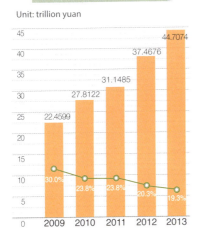

Fixed Assets Investment

Unit: trillion yuan

2009	2010	2011	2012	2013
22.4599	27.8122	31.1485	37.4676	44.7074
30.0%	23.8%	23.8%	20.3%	19.3%

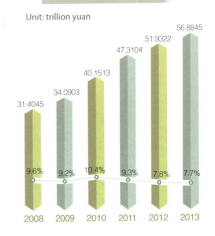

Gross Domestic Product

Unit: trillion yuan

2008	2009	2010	2011	2012	2013
31.4045	34.0903	40.1513	47.3104	51.9322	56.8845
9.6%	9.2%	10.4%	9.3%	7.8%	7.7%

Economic Structural Reform

A socialist market economy has taken shape in China, and is expected to be fully fledged by 2020.

Economic structural reform is the key for China to comprehensively deepen its reform, and the core problem lies in striking a balance between the role of the government and that of the market, allowing the market to play a decisive role in resource allocation and allowing the government to better play its own role.

Before 1978 China's economy was dominated by the public sector, with state-owned and collective-owned enterprises representing 77.6 percent and 22.4 percent, respectively, of all enterprises. The policy of reform and opening up has given wide scope to the development of various economic sectors. By now, almost all state-owned enterprises have adopted a corporate governance system. Their leveraging power, impact and leadership on the national economy has been constantly increasing.

At present, the economy features state ownership alongside the new mixed and private sectors. The state-owned sector dominates such fields as railways, civil aviation, posts and telecommunications, urban water, power and gas supplies, science and technology, education, national defense and finance. The private sector has grown swiftly, with many private firms moving away from traditional sectors like retail, foodstuffs, services and repairs to the knowledge and hi-tech industries.

Prosperous eateries

China's direction of deepening economic structural reform:

- To consolidate and develop the public sector of the economy; allow public ownership to take diverse forms; deepen the reform of state-owned enterprises, and improve the mechanisms for managing all types of state assets.
- To encourage, support and guide the development of the non-public sector, and ensure that economic entities under all forms of ownership have equal access to factors of production in accordance with the law, compete on a level playing field and are protected by the law as equals.
- To improve the modern market system and strengthen institutional procedures for setting macro-regulation targets and employing policy measures.
- To accelerate the reform of the fiscal and taxations systems, and improve the structure of the taxation system to promote social fairness.
- To establish a mechanism for equitable sharing of proceeds from public resource transfers.
- To deepen reform of the financial system and improve the modern financial system so that it will better contribute to macroeconomic stability and support the development of the real economy; and to speed up the development of private financial institutions, improve financial supervision and oversight, promote financial innovations and ensure financial stability.

GDP

| 2013 | 56.8845 trillion yuan |
| 2002 | 12.0333 trillion yuan |

Per Capita GDP

| 2013 | 41,804 yuan |
| 2002 | 9,398 yuan |

Economic Restructuring

Since it adopted the reform and opening up policy in 1978 China has given priority to light industry, increased the import of high-end consumer goods, strengthened the basic industries and infrastructure, and developed tertiary industry, so as to balance, upgrade and optimize its economic structure.

Carrying out strategic adjustment of the economic structure is the major goal of accelerating the change of the growth model.

Trial run of a machine in the workshop of Anhui Mechanical and Electrical Equipment Company

China's direction of economic restructuring:

◆ To boost domestic demand, speed up the establishment of a long-term mechanism for increasing consumer demand, unleash the potential of individual consumption, increase investment at a proper pace and expand the domestic market.

◆ To adopt policies and measures to better facilitate the development of the real economy, which should be a firm foundation of the economy. To promote the sound growth of strategic industries and advanced manufacturing industries, speed up the transformation and upgrading of traditional industries.

◆ To develop the next-generation information infrastructure and modern IT industry, better ensure information security, and promote the application of information network technologies.

◆ To enhance the core competitiveness of large and medium-sized enterprises and support the development of small and micro businesses, especially small and micro technology-based firms.

◆ To continue to implement the master strategy for regional development and fully leverage the comparative advantages of different regions. To give high priority to large-scale development of the western region, fully revitalize old industrial bases in northeast China, work vigorously to promote the rise of the central region, and support the eastern region in taking the lead in development.

◆ To make scientific plans for the scale and layout of urban agglomerations; and make small and medium-sized cities and small towns better able to develop industries, provide public services, create jobs, and attract population.

Innovation-driven Development

In over 30 years of reform and opening up, China's rapid economic development is mainly attributable to its low-cost labor force and resources. Entering the new development era, China formulated a new strategy of innovation-driven development.

This strategy covers the following aspects:

- To deepen reform of the system for managing science and technology, promote the close integration of science and technology with economic development. To establish a system of technological innovation in which enterprises play the leading role, the market points the way, and enterprises, universities and research institutes work together.
- To improve the knowledge-based innovation system, and enhance the research and capacity for applying research findings to production.
- To launch important national science and technology projects to remove major technological bottlenecks. To speed up the research, development and application of new technologies, products and production processes, strengthen innovation in integration of technologies and develop new business models.
- To improve standards for evaluating scientific and technological innovations and mechanisms for rewarding such innovations and applying them to production. To strengthen the protection of intellectual property rights. To efficiently allocate and fully integrate innovation resources.

 http://www.innofund.gov.cn
Since its establishment, the Innovation Fund for Small and Medium-sized Technology-based Firms (Innovation Fund) has guided social funds and other innovation resources to support the development of small and medium-sized technology-based firms through subsidies, subsidized loans and capital investment.

Electric vehicles being charged

All-round Opening Up

Port of Ningbo

China (Shanghai) Pilot Free Trade Zone

In August 2013 the State Council approved the setting up of China (Shanghai) Pilot Free Trade Zone as the first free trade zone on the Chinese mainland. On the following September 29, China (Shanghai) Pilot Free Trade Zone made its debut. Covering the Waigaoqiao Free Trade Zone as the core, Shanghai Pudong Airport and Yangshan Free Trade Port Area, the (Shanghai) Pilot Free Trade Zone is the new testing ground for the Chinese economy. Reform measures concerning transformation of government functions, financial system, trade and services, foreign investment and tax policies will be introduced to boost entrepot and offshore trade.

In 1978 when China began its economic structural reform, it also implemented a policy of gradual opening up. Since 1980 it has established five special economic zones along its coast, opened up 14 coastal cities in addition to a group of border cities and all provincial and regional capital cities, and set up bonded zones, state economic and technological development zones, and new- and hi-tech industrial development zones. The number of places opening up to the outside world has kept increasing, including economic zones, coastal cities, coastal economic zones, inland cities and those on big rivers, and border cities. These places, with different preferential policies, serve as windows with a radiating influence on inland areas, for developing an export-oriented economy, generating foreign exchange earnings through exports, and importing advanced technologies. Thus an omni-directional pattern of opening up, which is wide-ranging and multi-level with priorities, has basically taken shape.

On December 11, 2001, China officially joined the World Trade Organization (WTO), entering a new era of all-round opening up. The Chinese government, as promised, has changed the policy of opening up in certain areas to opening up in every possible area, opening sectors from traditional goods to services, and making market access more legitimate, transparent and standard.

China has been thus fully integrated into the world economy, opening its market, economy and society. In the economic sector it promotes the free flow of goods, services and factors of production across borders, and optimizes the resource distribution according to the law of the market, so as to internationalize production and consumption, liberalize trade and investment, and deregulate and internationalize the economic system.

Adapting to the trend of economic globalization, China has followed the international economic and political order and participated in international organizations in a broader scope and at a higher level, and actively plays its due role in these areas. China cooperates with both developing and developed countries, big and small; promotes South-South cooperation,

Xiamen Special Economic Zone

and South-North cooperation; propels economic, trade, technical and security cooperation; and improves the competitiveness of domestic enterprises and industries in participating in the international market and fending off external shocks and risks.

In August 2013 the Shanghai Pilot Free Trade Zone was set up, thereby unveiling new prospects for China's further opening up. In the meantime, a large number of key projects such as the Silk Road Economic Belt, 21st Century Maritime Silk Road and BCIM Economic Corridor are about to be launched, which will further expand the space for international economic cooperation.

Silk Road Economic Belt and 21st Century Maritime Silk Road

In September 2013, in a visit to Kazakhstan, Chinese president Xi Jinping stated that in order to build closer economic ties between European and Asian countries, and deepen mutual cooperation and development, the two sides should jointly build the Silk Road Economic Belt. In October 2013 Xi noted in a speech delivered to the Indonesian Parliament that China was willing to strengthen marine cooperation with ASEAN countries, make good use of the China-ASEAN marine cooperation fund set up by China, develop a sound marine cooperative partnership and jointly build the 21st Century Maritime Silk Road. Against the background of economic globalization, Chinese leaders put forward the strategy of building new Silk Roads to link China more closely with Eurasian, South-East Asian and other countries to raise their cooperation to a new level and bring harmony and prosperity to these countries and regions.

The 2000th McDonald's on China's mainland opened in Tianjin, April 2014

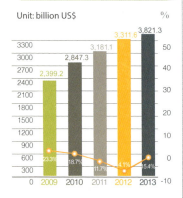

Utilizing Foreign Capital

China utilizes foreign capital mainly through three channels:

◆ 1) foreign loans, in the forms of loans from foreign governments, international financial institutions and foreign commercial banks, export credits, and issuance of bonds overseas;

◆ 2) direct foreign investment – Sino-foreign equity joint ventures, Sino-foreign cooperative joint ventures, wholly foreign-owned enterprises and Sino-foreign cooperative development projects; and

◆ 3) other foreign investment, by way of international leasing, compensation trade, processing and assembly, and issuance of stocks overseas.

Over the past 30 years or so, China's utilization of foreign capital has kept its momentum, with foreign direct investment as the major form. Since the 1980s the NPC and the State Council have promulgated a series of foreign-related laws and regulations, providing a legal basis and guarantee for foreign investment in China. So far, China has basically finished the revision of its foreign-related laws and regulations in accordance with its commitments to and the rules of the WTO. China has been hailed by world investors and financial sectors as one of the countries with best investment environment and potential.

Foreign Trade

In 2013 China's total import and export volume was US$4.16 trillion-worth, an increase of 7.6 percent over the previous year. Currently, China has trade relations with over 230 countries and regions. In 2013 China's five-largest trading partners were the EU, US, ASEAN, Hong Kong and Japan.

The major characteristics of China's foreign trade:

◆ Trade partners are more diversified: Trade volume in traditional markets such as Europe, US and Japan is declining while ASEAN and some other emerging markets are becoming new growth points.

◆ The layout of trade regions is more balanced: Foreign trade in Guangdong, Jiangsu, Shanghai, Beijing, Zhejiang, Shandong and Fujian is declining, while that in the central and western regions is increasing.

◆ The structure of foreign trade bodies is more rational: The proportion of private enterprises is increasing and that of foreign-funded enterprises is decreasing.

◆ The import-export commodity mix is becoming optimized: Exports of electrical and mechanical products and labor-intensive products is increasing steadily, and the import of consumer goods and

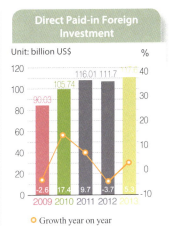

Digital controlled lathes made in Lu'an, Anhui Province, are sold worldwide.

resource products is increasing rapidly.

- The ability to conduct foreign trade is increasing: General trade is increasing while processing trade is decreasing.

Overseas Investment

China is emerging as a major investor worldwide. Its direct foreign investment is worth over $300 billion in over 170 countries and regions, involving export trade, catering and simple processing to marketing networks, shipping logistics, resource exploration, manufacturing and design development. Transnational mergers and acquisitions are the major forms of China's foreign investment.

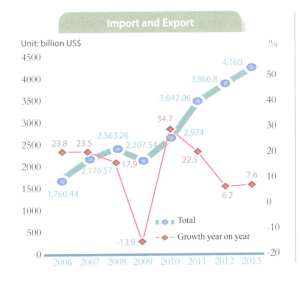

Free Trade Zone

A free trade zone is an area that covers every aspect of tariff of the parties concerned, as designated in agreements signed by two or more countries or regions and based on most-favored-nation status. In this area markets are further opened, tariff and non-tariff barriers are gradually abolished, market entry standards in service sectors are improved, and trade and investment are liberalized. China has 18 free-trade zones under construction, involving 31 countries and regions.

http://www.mofcom.gov.cn/

The Ministry of Commerce under the State Council is responsible for domestic and foreign trade and international economic cooperation.

Some large enterprises and groups have become multinationals with relatively strong international competitiveness, through specialized, intensive and scaled transnational management, widening of resource configuration and strengthening of capability to participate in overseas economic cooperation. Such group companies include China Petrochemical Company (Sinopec Group), State Grid Corporation of China and China National Petroleum Corporation (CNPC).

Coordinated Development of All Regions

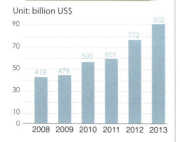

The reform and opening up policy, starting in 1978, has brought about great changes to and promoted the development of the eastern region of China. The implementation of the "Develop the West," "Revitalize the Northeast" and "Rise of Central China" strategies, and the establishment of "state pilot zones for overall reform" have promoted balanced development and comprehensive reform.

"Develop the West"

In 2000 China launched its "Develop the West" campaign. The western region includes Gansu, Guizhou, Qinghai, Shaanxi, Sichuan and Yunnan provinces, Tibet, Xinjiang Uygur, Guangxi Zhuang, Inner Mongolia and Ningxia Hui autonomous regions, and Chongqing Municipality. It accounts for over 70 percent of China's total land area and nearly 30 percent of its total population. Western China, bordering on 13 countries, is rich in land resources and mineral reserves. Hence it is believed to be the next golden area for opening up, after the east coast.

Over the decade, major infrastructure construction in transportation, water conservancy and energy tapping has been strengthened, initiating 20 new key projects with a total investment of 326.5 billion yuan, and thus quickening the pace of the development of inland and border areas.

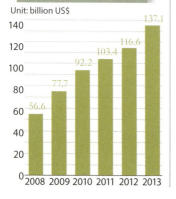

"Revitalize the Northeast"

In 2003 the CPC Central Committee and the State Council put forward the strategy to revitalize the old industrial bases in northeast China.

Measures such as social security and VAT reform, exemption from enterprise taxes in arrears, and policy-mandated bankruptcy of state-owned enterprises helped solve the deep-rooted institutional and structural problems there, revealing the region's great potential for development.

At present, continued efforts are being made to implement the strategy, pilot projects to relocate and transform old urban industrial districts and independent mining districts have been launched, and plans to rearrange and transform old industrial bases nationwide and ensure the sustainable development of resource-based cities are being formulated.

Construction site of Aksu-Kashgar Expressway on the Gobi desert

"Rise of Central China"

In order to promote the rapid growth of the six provinces (Shanxi, Jiangxi, Henan, Hubei, Hunan and Anhui) in central China, China in 2004 put forward the strategy of "Rise of Central China." This strategy aims to improve the grain-production capacity in this area, cultivate bases for coal and quality raw materials production, and construct an integrated transportation system. Currently, the agglomeration effect in city clusters along the middle reaches of the Yangtze River and economic zones of central China is being revealed, and the construction of industrial transfer model areas is going smoothly.

Reform Pilot Zone

China has set up some "state pilot zones for overall reform" to further explore how to build a harmonious society, innovate a regional development mode, and improve regional and national competitiveness. Different from the "special economic zones" designated in Shenzhen and other places after 1978, these state pilot zones are aimed at conducting comprehensive reform in some typical areas so as to provide new experiences and thoughts for the reforms in the economic, political and cultural structures across the country.

State Pilot Zones for Overall Reform

By the end of April 2013, the State Council had ratified 11 state-level pilot zones for overall reforms: Shanghai Pudong New Area, Tianjin Binhai New Area and Shenzhen; for coordinated reform of rural and urban areas in Chongqing and Chengdu; for building a resource-saving and environment-friendly society in Wuhan and the Changsha-Zhuzhou-Xiangtan conurbation; for new industrialization in Shenyang; for transformation of the resource-based economy in Shanxi Province; for enhancing cross-Straits exchanges and cooperation in Xiamen; and for overall reform of modern agriculture in Heilongjiang Province.

China's first chemical engineering base in Jilin Province, after snow

Agriculture

http://www.moa.gov.cn/
The Ministry of Agriculture under the State Council is responsible for agriculture and rural economic development.

With only 7 percent of the world's cultivated land, China successfully feeds one fifth of the world's population. Given a rural population of 900 million, the Chinese government has all along set as its top priority the solving of the issues related to agriculture, rural areas and farmers.

Since the introduction of the reform and opening up policy, China has established a two-tier management system that integrates unified and separated management on the basis of household contract management, opened up the markets for agricultural products in an all-round way and given agricultural tax exemptions and direct subsidies to farmers, initially shaping a rural economic system suited to the national conditions and geared to the needs of developing productivity. China has steadily increased grain yields and added variety to the supply of agricultural products, and has greatly improved rural incomes and made remarkable achievements in poverty alleviation. The government has gradually expanded the social security system and a new cooperative medical system in rural areas, and popularized nine-year compulsory education. Small towns have developed rapidly, while rural markets have flourished, and a large rural labor force has found non-agricultural employment, with millions of

Combine-harvester reaping the harvest, Guanghan, Sichuan Province, May 2014

rural migrant workers becoming an important part of China's industrial workforce. Industrialization, urbanization, modernization and social undertakings have accelerated in rural areas.

China leads the world in the output of grain, cotton, oil-bearing crops, fruit, meat, eggs, aquatic products and vegetables. With the continuous growth in the import and export trade of agricultural products, aquatic products, vegetables and fruit have become competitive farm products with a net export.

Expanding the scale of agricultural industrialization and promoting the all-round modernization of agriculture have been important factors in enhancing agricultural competitiveness in recent years. Now a pattern has been formed, spearheaded by some 600 key national enterprises, over 2,000 key provincial enterprises and a number of agencies connecting farmers with production bases. A large number of villages and towns in east China have already become specialized in export-oriented production, and many specialize in crop cultivation and stock breeding in central and western regions.

China's strategy to integrate urban and rural development:

◆ To continue to encourage industry to support agriculture in return for agriculture's earlier contribution to its development and encourage cities to support rural areas. To give more to farmers, take less from them and lift restrictions on their economic activities. To increase policy support for agriculture, benefit farmers and increase rural prosperity.

◆ To speed up the development of modern agriculture, raise the overall production capacity of agriculture, and ensure food security and effective supply of major agricultural products.

◆ To give high priority to rural areas in developing infrastructure and social programs. To work harder to build new rural areas, carry out programs of poverty alleviation

Agriculture, Rural Areas and Farmers

The three issues related to agriculture, rural areas and farmers highlight the problems faced by farmers engaged in crop planting, and livestock and poultry breeding, improvement of their living conditions, development of agriculture and social progress. These issues have long been the focus of the government. In the government work report made by Li Keqiang, premier of the State Council, these issues were listed as the No.1 priority for agricultural work in 2014.

Integrating Urban and Rural Development

The dual structure in urban and rural economic and social management evolving from the planned economy is a major institutional obstacle to solving the three issues related to agriculture, rural areas and farmers.

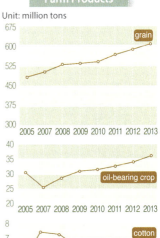

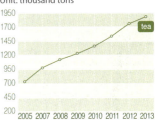

Modern agriculture of Beidahuang or "Great Northern Wilderness" in northeast China

CHINA

Yuan Longping

Yuan Longping, internationally known as the "father of hybrid rice," rewrote the history of rice-growing in China in the second half of the 20th century. His super-hybrid rice (12,000 kg per ha) is being promoted on a large scale.

through development, and improve overall rural working and living conditions.

◆ To improve the basic system for rural operations and protect in accordance with the law farmers' rights to farm the land they have contracted, to use the land on which their houses sit, and to share in the proceeds from rural collective operations, and strengthen the collective economy.

◆ To speed up improvements to institutions and mechanisms for promoting integrated urban and rural development, with the focus on integrating urban and rural planning, infrastructure and public services, to develop a new type of relationship in which industry promotes agriculture, urban areas support rural development, agriculture and industry benefit each other, and urban and rural development is integrated.

Terraced fields in Yuanyang County, Yunnan Province

Industry

A large-scale hydro generator

 http://www.miit.gov.cn

The Ministry of Industry and Information Technology is responsible for formulating the overall plans, policies and criteria of the information industry, supervising the daily operation of the industry, promoting the upgrading and innovation of major technical equipment, managing the communications industry, advancing the application of information technology and ensuring national information security.

New Path of Industrialization

Since the adoption of the reform and opening up policy, China's industry has realized leapfrog development, and reached a new peak in overall economic strength and restructuring efforts, laying a solid foundation for the country's transition to a manufacturing power.

China stresses integration of IT application and industrialization, and follows the new path of industrialization with Chinese characteristics, featuring scientific and technological progress, good economic returns, low resource consumption and little environmental pollution, together with a full display of its advantages in human resources.

Comprehensive and complete modern industrial and communications systems have been set up, with a solid support

Power grid construction

 From "Made in China" to "Created by China"

China's new and hi-tech industry is developing rapidly, becoming the new growth point in its industrial and economic development. As a new term, "created by China" is taking the place of "made in China" and being gradually recognized the world over. It conveys the concept of high-level creative brain work rather than simple manual labor. Through assimilating and renovating the technologies introduced, and large-scale technical upgrading, together with the aid of foreign investment, industrial enterprises are improving their production capability, making breakthroughs in a group of key projects and producing more domestically-made key equipment. Technical innovations are improved constantly and industrial technology upgrading is proving fruitful. Innovation capacity building is making headway in the national engineering laboratories, national engineering research centers, technical centers of enterprises, and similar institutions. Efforts have been made to protect IPR, and a standard management system has been established.

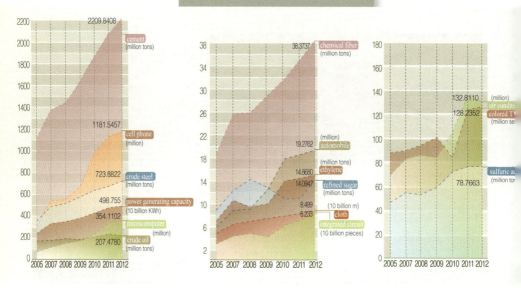

Workers of Sichuan Railway Group Cement Co at a construction site

chain encompassing fields such as raw materials and energy, equipment, consumption, science and technology for national defense and electronic information, of industrial goods with advanced production capability and world-leading output.

Raw Materials Industry

In 2012 the crude steel output of the Chinese mainland was 716 million tons, taking up 46.3 percent of the world's total. China is now the largest producer and consumer of nonferrous metals in the world. Since 2001 the output of 10 nonferrous metals in China has ranked first in the world. China is the biggest producer, user and exporter of rare earths. In chemical engineering, China has earmarked three regions for specialization in phosphate fertilizer production – in Yunnan, Guizhou and Hubei provinces – and launched potash projects in Qinghai Province and Xinjiang Uygur Autonomous Region, each with a production capacity of one million tons. All this has made China a big producer and consumer of petrochemicals, with the output of many of its products leading the world.

Equipment Industry

The equipment industry has become one of the largest industries in China. In 2013 the output value of China's equipment industry exceeded two trillion yuan, taking up over one third of the world's total and ranking top in the world. The output of most of China's equipment products ranks top in the world.

Significant progress has been made in China's emerging industries such as intelligent manufacturing equipment, ocean engineering equipment, advanced rail equipment and new-energy vehicles. The output value of China's high-end equipment manufacturing sector takes up over 10 percent of the equipment industry.

Consumer Goods Industry

In the past 30 years, the aggregate export value of China's textile products exceeded $2 trillion. The outputs of over 100 products, such as bicycles, sewing machines, batteries and beer, rank top in the world. China's household appliances, leather goods, furniture, down products, porcelain and bicycles take up over 50 percent of the international market.

A worker processes textile export products.

Chinese weaving enjoys a worldwide reputation. Its outputs of chemical fibers, yarn, cloth, wool fabrics, silk and garments rank top in the world. Its production of cotton accounts for a quarter of the world's total, and that of chemical fibers, half of the world's total. The textile industry is one of China's most competitive industries. Large textile enterprises employ a total of 20 million workers, thereby contributing greatly to job creation.

Aeronautics

As the fifth country to independently develop and launch man-made satellites and the third to master satellite recovery technology, China is one of the world's frontrunners in such important technological fields as satellite recovery, carrying of multiple satellites on one rocket, rocket technology, and testing and operation of stationary-orbit satellites. Great achievements have been made in the manufacturing and application of remote-sensing and communication satellites, and manned spacecraft. These achievements serve all aspects of the national economy.

The *Shenzhou-10* manned spacecraft, launched in June 2013, realized space rendezvous and docking with *Tiangong-1*, confirming that China's manned aviation had entered the research and development stage for space lab and space station projects. The *Chang'e-3* was launched from the Xichang Satellite Launch Center together with China's first lunar rover as the first spacecraft to soft-land on the Moon.

Astronauts of *Shenzhou-10* spacecraft saluting the public with their reentry capsule, June 26, 2013

A picture of moon rover *Yutu* taken by moon lander *Chang'e-3*, marking the success of the second phase of China's Lunar Exploration Program

So far, China has developed 12 models of the *Long March* carrier rocket series, and set up three launching sites in Jiuquan, Xichang and Taiyuan, making it one of the few countries capable of space-based telemetry, tracking and command (TT&C). Aerospace technology in China has evolved into a space research system and production and experimental base devoted to the development of carrier rockets and application satellites guided by high technology.

Adhering to the principle of mutual respect, mutual benefit and cooperation, and peaceful utilization of outer space for common development, China is willing to conduct wider cooperation with all friendly states to better utilize outer space for the benefit of mankind.

Information Industry

The information industry has become an industrial mainstay in China. In 2013 the sales revenue of China's information industry totaled 12.4 trillion yuan, with 3.1 trillion yuan contributed by software and information technology service industries. The development of products such as mobile intelligent terminals is accelerating, information consumption is increasing rapidly and e-commerce is already worth 10.67 trillion yuan.

The government is making efforts to improve the fiber-optic broadband network, focusing on access for each household. China Telecom has started to provide 8M access bandwidth to all cities; each township has 2M access capacity, and 100M fiber-optic broadband access is being installed in some large cities. So far, China has 10 million fiber-optic broadband subscribers, among whom 100,000 are home users.

The Beidou satellite navigation system is a global system that China has developed and is operating independently. The Beidou system is expected to cover the entire world by 2020. In March 2014, the Chinese government used 10 satellites of the Beidou satellite navigation system to search for the wreckage of Malaysian Airlines Flight 370.

http://www.cmse.gov.cn/

China Manned Space Engineering Project or Project 921 was approved by the Chinese government on September 21, 1992. In order to strengthen the project management, China Manned Space Engineering Office (CMSEO) is set up to exercise administrative functions on behalf of the government.

Number of Netizens and Internet Coverage Rate in China

Life vests with Beidou satellite navigation device were used in a maritime search-and-rescue and fire drill, Shandong

Number of Websites in China
Unit: million

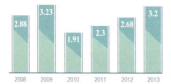

Note: The websites of the *EDU* and *CN* domains are excluded.

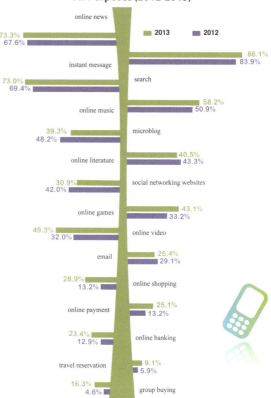

Proportion of Cell Phone Netizens for All Purposes (2012-2013)

Purpose	2013	2012
online news	73.3%	67.6%
instant message	86.1%	83.9%
search	73.0%	69.4%
online music	58.2%	50.9%
microblog	39.3%	48.2%
online literature	40.5%	43.3%
social networking websites	30.9%	42.0%
online games	43.1%	33.2%
online video	49.3%	32.0%
email	25.4%	29.1%
online shopping	28.9%	13.2%
online payment	25.1%	13.2%
online banking	23.4%	12.9%
travel reservation	9.1%	5.9%
group buying	16.3%	4.6%

Service Industry

Supermarket staff arranging fruits

The rapid development of the service industry, particularly the modern types, is a salient feature in the process of China's industrial restructuring. Significant development has been achieved in the traditional service sectors such as transportation, wholesale and retail, and catering. To adapt to the demands of industrialization, urbanization, deregulation of the market, IT application and internationalization, modern service sectors, including finance, insurance, real estate, consultancy, e-commerce, modern logistics and tourism, are making great strides, improving the overall quality of China's service industry.

In 2013 the proportion of the tertiary industry in the three types of industry rose to 46.1 percent, overtaking secondary industry for the first time, a sign of the further optimization of China's industrial structure. China's service industry still lags behind those of developed countries. The Chinese government is prioritizing the development of the service industry in upgrading the industrial structure to balance the three types of industry and trying to increase the proportion of the service industry in the GDP to 55 percent by 2015.

Transportation

In recent years, China's transportation networks and passenger and freight traffic volumes have maintained rapid growth.

Highways

Highways are China's key infrastructure sector. By the end of 2012 the total length of highways had reached 4.2375 million km.

The construction of expressway witnesses a momentum of rapid development. By the end of 2012, the total length of expressways nationwide had reached 96,200 km. According to the National Expressway Network Plan, China will build an expressway system connecting all provincial capitals with Beijing and each other, linking major cities as well as important counties.

National Expressway 30 that links Sayram Lake and Guozi Valley: the first expressway in the mountainous area of Xinjiang

Total Lengths of All Grades of Highways

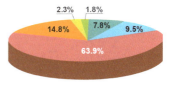

- Expressway, 96,200 km
- Grade I, 74,300 km
- Grade II, 331,500 km
- Grade III, 401,900 km
- Grade IV, 2,705,800 km
- Substandard, 627,900 km

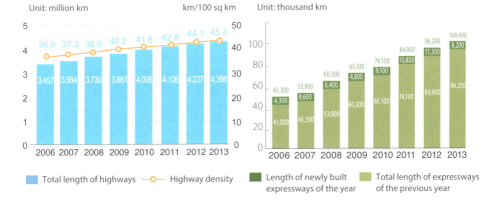

Qinghai-Tibet Railway

Railways

In recent years China's railway construction has experienced unprecedented development in terms of scale, construction standards and speed. In 2006 the Qinghai-Tibet Railway was completed and opened to traffic. It is the highest and longest plateau railway in the world. In 2010 the Datong-Qinhuangdao Railway broke the world freight capacity record, with its annual freight carriage exceeding 400 million tons. By the end of 2013 China's railway mileage in operation had reached 100,000 km.

China invests heavily in building high-speed railways. Put into operation on December 26, 2012, the Beijing-Guangzhou High-speed Railway is the longest high-speed railway line in the world, with a total length of about 2,200 km. By the end of 2013 the length of China's high-speed railways had exceeded 10,000 km, with another 12,000 km under construction.

The first train on Wuhan-Guangzhou High-speed Railway pulling out from Wuhan

China has become the country with the fastest-growing and longest mileage, highest running speed and largest building scale, and employing the most comprehensive technology in the railways sector. It is estimated that by 2020 the total length of China's railway lines with a maximum speed of 200 km/h and above will exceed 18,000 km, accounting for more than half of the world's total mileage of high-speed railway lines.

China has basically completed a nationwide rapid-transit network for passenger traffic within the framework of four north-south and four east-west high-speed railways, thus forming a one-to-eight-hour transportation radius for the whole country with Beijing as its center. China's provincial and autonomous regional capital cities, excluding Urumqi, Lhasa and Haikou, have all been included in this rapid-transit circle. As the high-speed railways are linked into a network, traveling by train is as convenient as traveling by bus, as on-the-spot ticket service is available, and its travel environment approaches civil aviation standards.

Total Length of Railways and Electrified Mileage

Unit: thousand km
- Railways in operation
- Electrified mileage

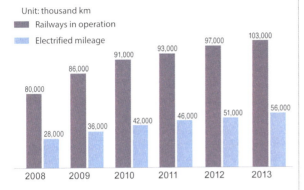

Volume of Railway Passenger Transportation

Unit: billion

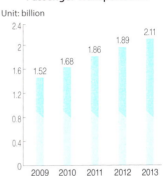

Light Rail Transit

In recent years, the government has increased its investment in the construction of LRT (light rail transit) to lessen the pressure on urban transportation. LRT systems have been put into use in large cities like Beijing, Tianjin, Shanghai, Chongqing, Guangzhou, Dalian and Nanjing. It is estimated that a total of 2,000 km of light rail lines will be in operation by 2020, and 4,500 km by 2050. By then, these LRTs will be integrated with subways, suburban railways and other rail systems, to form a rapid transportation system, taking 50 percent to 80 percent of the total load of urban public transportation.

Volume of Railway Freight

Unit: billion tons

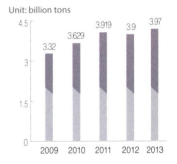

Line 3, Changchun Light Rail Transit, the first of its kind on China's mainland

CHINA

The volume of freight on the Yangtze River reached 1.92 billion tons in 2013, breaking the world record for the 7th successive year.

Ports

China has invested in the construction of ports along the Yangtze and Pearl rivers, and the Beijing-Hangzhou Grand Canal. Remarkable achievements in port building have become the locomotive for the operations of harbors and regional economic development.

Among the 16 ports each with a yearly freight volume exceeding 100 million tons, those of Shanghai, Shenzhen, Qingdao, Tianjin, Guangzhou, Xiamen, Ningbo and Dalian are listed among the world's top 50 container ports. The Port of Shanghai holds the first position in the world in this regard. In 2013 the Port of Shenzhen became the world's third-largest container port after those of Shanghai and Singapore.

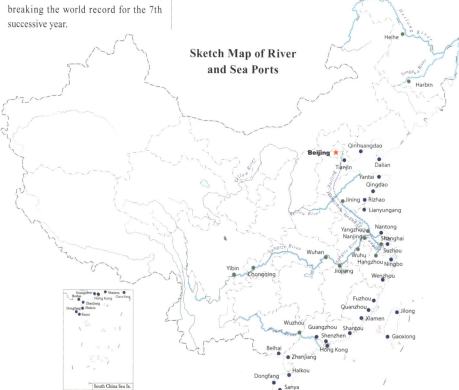

Sketch Map of River and Sea Ports

Civil Aviation

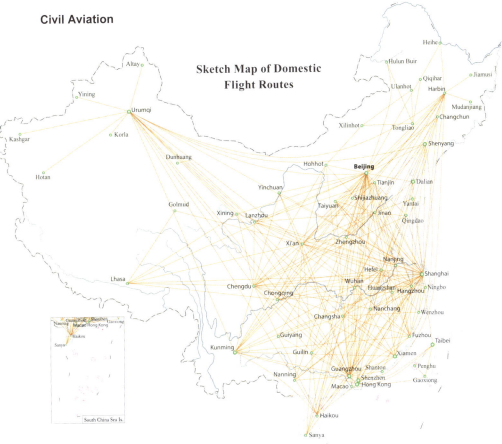

In recent years China's civil aviation routes and network have been further improved. By the end of 2013 there were 193 civil airports nationwide. Among them, 24 have an annual passenger throughput of over 10 million. Domestic airlines fly to 114 cities in 49 countries.

China's civil aviation is expanding fast and has the second-biggest air transportation system in the world. Air transportation has become a popular way of traveling. In 2013 a total of 325 million passengers and 5.57 million tons of cargo and mail were transported by air.

Chinese civil airlines are mainly state-run, including Air China, Southern Airlines, China Eastern Airlines and Hainan Airlines, but government backing is being given to private and Sino-foreign jointly owned airlines.

Terminal 3 of Shenzhen Airport was opened on November 28, 2013.

Finance and Insurance

Internet Finance

Internet finance refers to conducting financial transactions such as capital flow, payment and information intermediaries through Internet tools such as e-pay, cloud computing, social network services and search engines.

In 2013, against the background of financial reform, innovation in Internet finance took place at an incredible speed, and the emergence of Alipay, crowd funding, group purchase of financial products, and peer-to-peer lending made Internet finance even more popular.

Traditional financial institutions also actively use the Internet to make adjustments to revitalize the industry, which has given rise to the emergence of online loans, big data financing, financial portal websites, third-party payment, crowd funding and online financial information services.

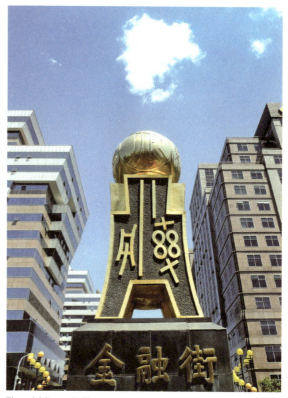
Financial Street, Beijing

Financial System

China has basically formed a financial system under the regulation, control and supervision of the central bank, with state banks as the mainstay, featuring the separation of policy-related banks and commercial banks, and the cooperation of various financial institutions with mutually complementary functions. At the same time, China's Internet financial sector is enjoying a sound momentum of development.

Banking

The banking industry is in the forefront of China's finance industry. China's banks at the present stage fall into three categories: the central bank, commercial banks and policy-related banks.

The People's Bank of China (PBOC) exercises the power and function of the central bank, being responsible for making monetary policies, issuing currency and handling reserves of foreign exchange and gold. The Industrial and Commercial Bank of China (ICBC), Bank of China (BOC), Agricultural Bank of China (ABC) and Construction Bank of China (CBC) are state-owned commercial banks. The Agricultural Development Bank of China, China Development Bank and China Import and Export Bank were once policy-related banks. China Development Bank has now changed into a shareholding commercial bank, and China Import and Export Bank is nearly completing its reform.

People's Bank of China, Beijing

China has over 100 urban commercial banks, more than 1,000 urban credit cooperatives and a large number of rural credit cooperatives. There are about 200 foreign financial institutions operating in China, more than 80 of which are allowed to handle transactions in China's currency, the renminbi (RMB).

The reform of financial institutions has made breakthroughs. The BOC, the CBC, the ICBC and the ABC have been transformed into shareholding institutions, allowing them to be listed on the Hong Kong and Shanghai stock exchanges. Through reform, their market value, profitability and capital savings rank among the world's leaders.

Foreign-funded banks in Shanghai

Currency and Exchange Rates

The RMB is issued and controlled solely by the PBOC. RMB exchange rates are decided by the PBOC and announced by the State Administration of Foreign Exchange, the latter exercising the functions and powers of exchange control.

The RMB experienced the changes from a single exchange rate, multiple exchange rate to single exchange rate again. China's exchange rate policy has been consistent and responsible, committed to the reform of the RMB exchange rate. China will adhere to three principles in its currency policy: Any change must be controlled, it must be on the government's own initiative and any shift must be gradual. Guided by these principles, China will improve its managed floating exchange rate system, give full play to the role of the market, increase the flexibility of the RMB exchange rate and maintain the currency's stability at an appropriate level. China carries out bilateral currency exchanges with the ROK, Malaysia, Belarus, Indonesia and Argentina.

Bank clerk taking deposits

An absorbed stock investor

Securities

In 1990 and 1991 China set up securities exchanges in Shanghai and Shenzhen, respectively. Over the past 20 years or so, the Chinese stock market has completed a journey that took many countries 100 years or more to make.

As for ordinary citizens, the stock market has joined bank deposits as the main channel for investment.

Today, a network system for securities exchange account settlement has been formed, with the Shanghai and Shenzhen exchanges as the powerhouses, radiating to all parts of the country. Relevant technology has reached advanced international standards, with the realization of paperless trading.

With 10 years' efforts, Growth Enterprise Market was born in October 2009. In 2012, the eye-catching Growth Enterprise Delisting System, the first such system in the history of A share market in real sense was released. In December 2013, with the National Equities Exchange and Quotations services expanding nationwide, this Over-The-Counter capital market known as China's NASDAQ became a bonanza for those small and medium-sized enterprises.

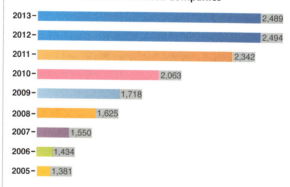

Insurance

The insurance industry in China was resumed in 1980, after 20 years of suspension. China's insurance companies are actively exploring the international market, setting up operations and representative offices in Southeast Asia, Europe and North America.

Tourism

Tourism market

China's tourism market has grown rapidly. In 2013, domestic tourists recorded 3.26 billion visits, an increase of 10.3 percent over the previous year; the revenue from domestic tourism totaled 2.6276 trillion yuan, an increase of 15.7 percent over the previous year; inbound tourist trips were 129.08 million; foreign currency receipts from international tourism was US$51.7 billion, an increase of 3.3 percent over the previous year; overseas trips made by Chinese tourists were 98.19 million, an increase of 18 percent over the previous year.

Summer Palace, Beijing

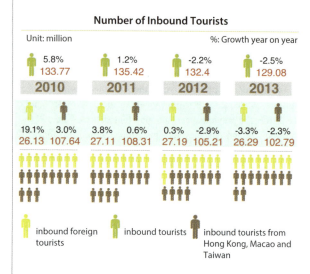

The Chinese people on average make 1.5 trips each year, and the country receives 50 million inbound tourists staying for over one night, the third-highest rate in the world. China has approved 146 countries and regions as tourist destinations for Chinese citizens at their own expense, and 114 of them have started package tour services.

Tourism Services

The rapid development of China's transportation infrastructure has provided safe and convenient transportation for both overseas and domestic tourists. All large or medium-sized cities and scenic spots have hotels with full facilities and services.

China has about 20,000 travel agencies, 2,000 of which are capable of providing services for inbound tourists and 1,070 for outbound services. In 2003 the Chinese government allowed the establishment of foreign-controlled or foreign-funded travel agencies. So far, China has over 20 foreign-controlled or foreign-funded travel agencies.

China has 110 famous cultural cities each with a history of over 1,000 years, and 339 excellent tourism cities. It is home to 56 ethnic groups, with diverse cultures and customs. In Yunnan, Guizhou, Sichuan, Guangxi, Hunan, Hubei, Gansu, Ningxia, Tibet, Inner Mongolia and Xinjiang, which have large minority communities, it is possible to view a great variety of folk cultures and customs.

In October 2013 China's first Tourism Law came into effect.

Villages of Miao people in Xijiang, Guizhou Province

中 国　C h i n a

Ecological conservation is a long-term task vital to the wellbeing of the people and the future of the nation. China is a developing country with the largest population in the world. In the process of sustained and rapid economic growth, the environmental problems that emerged by stages in developed countries during their centuries-long industrialization are breaking out in China all at once. China's development is confronting increasing environmental problems.

To address these problems, the CPC's 18th National Congress broached new ideas and requirements for ecological progress and environmental protection, pointing the way to building a beautiful China and achieving sustainable development of the Chinese nation.

Environmental
Protection

- Laws and Systems for Environmental Protection
- Coping with Climate Change
- Air Pollution Control
- Water Pollution Control
- Forest Protection
- Wetland Protection
- Marine Protection
- Nature Reserves
- Protecting Endangered Animals and Plants
- ENGOs
- International Cooperation

Laws and Systems for Environmental Protection

People lay straw grids in the Badain Jaran Desert to control desertification and prevent sandstorms.

The Chinese Constitution specifies that "The state protects and improves the environment in which people live and the ecological environment. It prevents and controls pollution and other public hazards." Environmental protection has been a basic national policy since the 1980s. The first Environmental Protection Law was issued in 1989. Following that, more laws and regulations, including the Energy Conservation Law, Renewable Energy Law and Circular Economy Promotion Law, have been promulgated to refine the environmental protection legal system. Furthermore, central and local systems of environmental protection standards have been set up. In 2008 the State Environmental Protection Administration was upgraded to the Ministry of Environmental Protection.

China has adopted an environmental management system

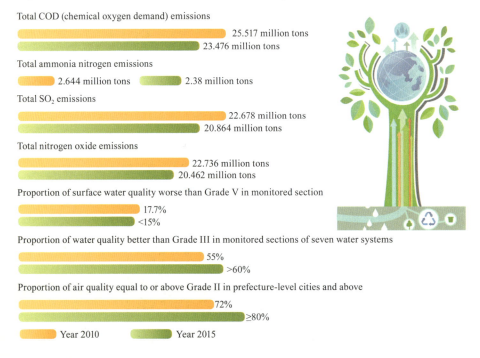

Major Environmental Protection Indices in the 12th Five-year Plan (2011-2015)

Total COD (chemical oxygen demand) emissions
- 25.517 million tons
- 23.476 million tons

Total ammonia nitrogen emissions
- 2.644 million tons
- 2.38 million tons

Total SO$_2$ emissions
- 22.678 million tons
- 20.864 million tons

Total nitrogen oxide emissions
- 22.736 million tons
- 20.462 million tons

Proportion of surface water quality worse than Grade V in monitored section
- 17.7%
- <15%

Proportion of water quality better than Grade III in monitored sections of seven water systems
- 55%
- >60%

Proportion of air quality equal to or above Grade II in prefecture-level cities and above
- 72%
- ≥80%

Year 2010　　Year 2015

with governments at all levels being accountable for local environmental quality, competent departments exercising supervision, and related departments administering in accordance with the law. A system of inter-ministerial joint meetings for environmental protection is in place, and representative offices for regional environmental protection supervision have been set up to enhance coordination and cooperation between departments and regions.

Progress in China's Human Rights in 2012, a white paper issued by the Chinese government, put forward the concept of ecological human rights guarantee for the first time and includes ecological conservation in the scope of China's human rights guarantee, stressing that "China insists on building the ecological and civilized idea of respecting nature, complying with nature, and protecting nature, and highlights the significant position of the ecological civilization."

Coping with Climate Change

The Report of the 18th CPC National Congress defines the ecological conservation in a separate section and emphasizes the need to "strive for green, circular and low-carbon development" and to "build a beautiful China." Over the past decade, from Copenhagen, Durban to Warsaw, China has made solemn commitments at climate conferences and always kept its promises; by bringing up restrictive indicators in the 11th Five-year Plan (2006-2010), relocating and rectifying steel and iron plants and other high-consumption industries, controlling the sources of the sandstorms that afflict Beijing and Tianjin, putting forward energy-saving and emission-reducing plans, reducing the energy consumption per unit of GDP by 12.9 percent and steadily pushing forward the ecological compensation mechanism. China is gradually adopting the path of green development which can benefit future generations.

In 2006 China pledged to reduce its energy consumption per unit of GDP by 20 percent in 2010, compared to the figure for 2005. In 2007 China became the first developing country to set forth and carry out a national plan for coping with climate change. In 2009 China set its goal for reducing emis-

Public bicycle rentals, Beijing

Energy Saving and New Energy Vehicle Industry Development Plan

Following the release of the Energy Saving and New Energy Vehicle Industry Development Plan (2012-2020), Beijing, Shanghai and other cities enacted subsidy policies to promote sales of new energy vehicles. This encourages vehicle manufacturers to invest more in R&D of new energy vehicles. The new energy vehicle industry may become a new growth axis in China's future auto market. At the two eye-catching auto exhibitions in Beijing and Shanghai, new energy vehicles representing cutting edge technology have won the admiration of their peers.

China (Shanghai) International Technology Fair, April 25, 2014

sions of greenhouse gases per unit of GDP by 40 percent to 45 percent by 2020, compared to the figure for 2005. In addition, China has established a series of legally binding goals, including the reduction of emission of CO_2 per unit of GDP by 17 percent in 2015, compared to 2010, and the proportional increase of non-fossil energies in primary energy consumption to 11.4 percent.

China adheres to the double-track negotiation mechanism of the United Nations Framework Convention on Climate Change and the Kyoto Protocol, insisting on the principles of the leading position of contracting parties, transparency, widespread participation and consultation to give full play to the main channel of international negotiations on climate change within the framework of the UN.

In 2007 China attended the UN conference in Bali, Indonesia, making a substantial contribution to the promulgation of the Bali Road Map. In 2009 China took part in the Copenhagen Climate Conference, playing a significant role in breaking the negotiations impasse and urging all parties to reach an agreement.

In 2012, the Doha Climate Change Conference confirmed the second commitment period of the Kyoto Protocol on legal grounds, achieving a comprehensive outcome of promoting the implementation of the Protocol through long-term cooperation, adhering to the principle of "common but differentiated responsibilities," and maintaining the basic institutional framework of the United Nations Framework Convention and the Kyoto Protocol.

China released its National Strategy for Climate Change Adaptation at the Warsaw Climate Change Conference. This is China's first strategy targeting climate change adaptation. Xie Zhenhua, vice minister of the National Development and Reform Commission (NDRC), stated that China's position is open and transparent, and it is determined to cope with climate change more actively and intensify its efforts to save energy and reduce emissions.

China was the first developing country to implement a National Climate Change Program. It has formulated or revised the Energy Conservation Law, Renewable Energy Law, Circular Economy Promotion Law, Clean Production Promotion Law, Forest Law, Grassland Law and Regulations on Civil Building Efficiency. Laws and regulations are an important

The 6th China International Low Carbon Industry Exhibition was opened on April 2, 2014 at Beijing Exhibition Center. Pictured is an environment-friendly heating system.

means to address climate change.

China has made the most intensive efforts in energy conservation and emission reduction in recent years. It has improved the taxation system and advanced the pricing reform of resource products with a view to putting in place at an early date a pricing mechanism that is responsive to market supply and demand, resource scarcity and the costs of environmental damage. It has introduced major energy conservation projects and launched an energy conservation campaign, bringing energy-saving action to industry, transportation, construction and other key sectors of the economy. It has implemented pilot projects for a circular economy, promoted energy-saving and eco-friendly vehicles, and subsidized households to use energy-saving products. It has worked hard to shut down outdated production facilities that are energy-intensive and heavily polluting.

China has enjoyed the fastest growth in the world of new and renewable energy. On the basis of protecting the eco-environment, it has developed hydro power in an orderly way, and encouraged the exploitation of renewable energy, including solar and geothermal energy and wind power in the countryside, remote areas and other places with proper conditions. China has the largest area of man-made forests in the world, and it is continuing its large-scale endeavors to return farmland to forest and expand forestation.

 http://www.zhb.gov.cn/

Directly under the State Council, the Ministry of Environmental Protection is responsible for formulating and implementing plans, policies and standards concerning environmental protection, organizing and drawing up regional environmental function plans, supervising environmental pollution control, coordinating efforts to solve major problems concerning environmental protection, supervising the enforcement of laws and regulations, and coordinating cross-regional environmental affairs.

Air Pollution Control

China began to control air pollution in the 1970s, mainly by preventing the emergence of new sources of pollution, and by strengthening the control and management of existing pollution sources.

In the early 1970s it carried out a nationwide investigation on the quality of its air. In August 1973 it convened the First National Environmental Protection Meeting, and in December promulgated the Trial Standards for the Industrial "Three Wastes" Discharge, putting forward the "three-simultaneity" system that requires prevention and control facilities targeting environmental pollution and other public hazards for new, rebuilding or expansion projects be designed, constructed and put into use simultaneously with the main projects.

In April 2000 the revised Law on the Prevention and Control of Atmospheric Pollution approved at the 15th session of the Ninth NPC Standing Committee marked great progress

Wind-power generating units on prairie in Inner Mongolia Autonomous Region

made in China's efforts to prevent and control atmospheric pollution according to law. In May 2010 the General Office of the State Council released Instructions on the Joint Prevention and Control of Atmospheric Pollution to Improve Regional Air Quality. This was China's first comprehensive policy on prevention and control of air pollution, making 10 breakthroughs and innovations in policies and measures concerning environmental protection, and clarifying the guiding thought, goal and key measures for air pollution prevention and control in the coming period.

In 2012 China released the newly-amended Ambient Air Quality Standards, adding monitoring values for the limits of fine particles (PM2.5) and the density of O_3 within eight hours. In 2013 PM2.5 was first mentioned in the government report delivered by the State Council premier. Environmental issues including air quality management have become the most practical and pressing task for the Chinese government.

Since January 2013, many cities have been afflicted by smog, featuring moderate and even heavy pollution. Beijing has issued its first orange alert due to serious smog and taken measures to respond to extremely heavy pollution. Smog and sandstorms have severely affected the atmosphere, threatening people's health and traffic safety.

In the same year, the Chinese government adopted key measures to prevent and control air pollution, establishing a mechanism of joint prevention and control in the areas along the Bohai Bay, including Beijing, Tianjin and Hebei, and in the Yangtze River Delta and the Pearl River Delta, and bringing the goal of air control into the responsibility evaluation system – local governments must treat heavy air pollution as an emergency, restricting the production and waste discharges of key enterprises and limiting the use of vehicles according to pollution levels; the emission intensity of major pollutants in key industries is targeted to drop by over 30 percent by 2017.

The central government set up a special fund of 10 billion yuan in 2014 to substitute subsidies with rewards to address air pollution in key regions, formulate standards for "leaders" in energy efficiency and pollution emission control in key industries, and reward qualified enterprises. In the first three years of the 12th Five-year Plan period (2011-2015), China's environmental protection input increased by over 200 billion yuan every year.

Action Plan for Air Pollution Prevention and Control

The Action Plan for Air Pollution Prevention and Control released in 2013 was regarded as the strictest one ever made in history. Its targets are as follows: PM10 across the nation must decline by over 10 percent in 2017 compared with that in 2012. PM2.5 of the Beijing-Tianjin-Hebei, Yangtze River Delta and Pearl River Delta areas must drop by about 25 percent, 20 percent and 15 percent, respectively. The overall air quality must improve within five years, and environmental improvement will be taken into consideration in evaluation of officials.

Water Pollution Control

China started its first large-scale pollution control project – the pollution investigation and control of Beijing's Guanting Reservoir – in 1972. The project lasted eight years, and 112 pollution control programs were finished successively.

In August 1991 the State Environmental Protection Administration (now Ministry of Environmental Protection) and the Ministry of Construction (now Ministry of Housing and Urban-Rural Development) jointly held the Second National Meeting on Urban Environmental Protection. City governments at all levels were required to actively promote centralized pollution control, strengthen infrastructure, enhance protection of drinking water sources, and improve urban rivers and lakes. The comprehensive efforts had slowed the worsening of pollution in major cities, and some water environmental quality indices remained stable.

In February 1989 a pollution accident took place on the Huaihe River, threatening the lives of millions of people and causing economic losses worth more than 100 million yuan. In 1993 the State Council decided to take the Huaihe River as a key pollution control project, and carried out large-scale water basin treatment with "three rivers" (Huaihe, Haihe and Liaohe) and "three lakes" (Taihu, Chaohu and Dianchi) as the focus. This indicated that China's water pollution control had entered the phase of major river basin treatment.

Since 2003 the State Environmental Protection Administration has published annual updates on pollution control in key river basins and sea areas. Thanks to years of effort, there has been an obvious improvement in the water environment in the seriously polluted areas, and the Yellow River has not run dry for a dozen consecutive years.

In 2007 the state earmarked several billion yuan for the Water Body Pollution Control and Treatment Program, focusing on drinking water safety, environmental control of river basins and urban water pollution treatment. The work on drinking water safety in the countryside has been strengthened to supply drinkable water to 400 million rural people. The 12th Five-year Plan set such goals as controlling the total discharge of major pollutants, adopting a strict protection system

Waterfalls and a deep pond at Jiuzhaigou scenery area, Sichuan Province

of drinking water sources, strengthening pollution treatment in such sectors as papermaking, printing and dying, chemicals, leather manufacturing and large-scale livestock and poultry breeding, and continuing water pollution prevention and control in major river basins and regions to guarantee drinking water safety for urban and rural residents.

In July 2013 Premier Li Keqiang chaired a State Council executive meeting, studying and making plans to speed up the development of energy-conservation and environmental-protection industries, and boost information consumption, effective domestic demand, economic restructuring and upgrading. In 2014 the Action Plan for Water Pollution Prevention and Control will be released with the focus on industrial waste water treatment, and the aim of eliminating Grade V water before 2017, three years ahead of the target.

Forest Protection

Currently, China's forest area is 208 million ha, with a forest coverage area of 21.63 percent and forest reserves totaling 15.137 million cu m. While global forest resources are undergoing a decline, China has seen increases in forest resources for 30 consecutive years. By 2020 its forest coverage rate is expected to reach 23 percent. But China is still an ecologically fragile country with forest coverage which is far less than the average global level of 31 percent, as its per capita forest area is 1/4 of the world's average and per capita reserves of forests 1/7 of the world's total.

Since the 1950s China has made great strides in forest plantation, increasing the afforested area from 22 million ha to 69 ha, which ranks first in the world. While many countries have seen a decline in forest resources, China has seen increases in both area and reserves of its forests, and was listed by the United Nations Environmental Program as one of the 15 countries preserving the greatest area of forests. An effective program, starting in 1998, put an end to the felling of trees in natural forests nationwide. In many areas, erstwhile lumbermen have now become forest rangers.

Ensuring Safe Drinking Water for Farmers

At the World Summit on Sustainable Development, held in Johannesburg in 2002, the participants committed themselves to halving the proportion of people who lack clean water and proper sanitation by 2015. By the end of 2013 China had solved the problem of ensuring safe drinking water for over 400 million rural people, although there are still about 100 million Chinese people suffering from lack of drinkable water. The government work report in 2014 points out that the government will solve the problem of ensuring safe drinking water for another 60 million rural people this year, and for all rural people by the end of 2015.

A wooden path for tourists in Lhalu wetland, Tibet

Wetland Protection

As a key element of the Earth's three ecological systems, together with forest and ocean, wetlands play the role of the "kidney of the Earth." China is home to various types of wetland, with rich biodiversity. The total area of wetlands each larger than 100 ha is 38.48 million ha, ranking fourth in the world and first in Asia.

The Chinese government has adopted numerous measures to enhance protection of wetlands. In 1992 China joined the Ramsar Convention on Wetlands and has so far designated 46 international-level wetlands in accordance with the Convention. However, in recent years, improper utilization of wetlands has occurred, including invasion by projects and unsustainable reclamation. According to the Protection Evaluation of National Wetland Nature Reserves released by the Institute of Remote Sensing and Digital Earth of the Chinese Academy of Sciences in 2012, the total area of national wetland nature reserves had declined over the previous 30 years. The Regulation on Wetland Protection put into effect on May 1 2013 stipulates that other than under special permit by law, any activity threatening wetlands and their biological functions is totally banned, including reclamation, herding, fishing, sand and earth removal, mining, and discharge of domestic sewage and industrial waste water.

China's Wetlands

China has a total of 53.6026 million ha of wetlands, taking up 5.58 percent of the national land area. The natural wetland area is 46.6747 million ha, taking up 87.08 percent of the nation's total wetland area. China's wetland area has decreased by 8.82 percent, or 3.3963 million ha, in the past 10 years. Currently 23.2432 million ha of wetlands are under protection.

China has 4,220 varieties of wetland plants in 483 biomes, and 2,312 wetland vertebrates in 266 families, 51 catalogues and five classes, among which there are 231 varieties of wetland birds. Wetlands are a species gene pool.

Marine Protection

So far, more than 210 marine nature reserves of various kinds, including 33 national marine nature reserves, 23 special national marine reserves and 18 national ocean parks, have been established in China. They protect marine shoreline, estuary and island bio-environments that possess great value for science and education. They also protect endangered marine animals such as the Indo-Pacific hump-backed dolphin (Sousa chinensis) and their habitats, as well as typical oceanic eco-systems such as mangrove swamps, coral reefs and coastal wetlands.

By 2015, three new national marine nature reserves and 44 special national marine reserves will be set up as part of a national marine protection network.

The Law on Protection of the Ocean Environment covers the supervision and management of the ocean environment; surveying, monitoring, assessing and conducting of scientific research of the ocean environment; projects for control of ocean pollution; and the curbing of pollution dumping into the ocean. Marine ecological compensation practices will be carried out in typical seas in order to build a marine ecological compensation mechanism.

Observer in the Arctic Council

After a seven-year wait since it presented its application for observer status to the Arctic Council in 2006, China's dream came true in May 2013. In the 1990s China began to enhance its focus on and research into Arctic affairs, and dispatched its first Arctic scientific exploration team in 1999. So far the Chinese scientists have carried out five explorations. In 2004 China set up the Arctic Yellow River Station as its base camp for Arctic exploration.

Nature Reserves

China's first nature reserve was the Dinghu Mountain Nature Reserve, established in 1956 in Zhaoqing, Guangdong Province. By the end of 2013 there were 2,697 nature reserves of various kinds, accounting for more than 15 percent of the country's land territory and exceeding the world's average of 12 percent. Of them, 407 are state-level ones. Protected through these nature reserves is about 90 percent of China's land eco-systems, 85 percent of its wildlife population and nearly 65 percent of its higher plant communities.

Established in August 2000, the Sanjiangyuan Nature Reserve has the greatest concentration of biodiversity of all of China's nature reserves. Covering an area of 31.8 million ha and

Père David's deer at Dafeng Nature Reserve, Jiangsu Province

with an average elevation of 4,200 m, it is also the largest nature reserve in China. It is located in the central part of the Qinghai-Tibet Plateau, at the source of the Yangtze, Yellow and Lancang rivers. In 2005 state funds totaling 7.5 billion yuan were committed to the Sanjiangyuan protection and construction project. By the end of 2011, China's first national comprehensive ecological protection pilot zone was built in Sanjiangyuan as a prelude to higher-level protection and construction.

Guangdong Province has about 300 nature reserves, the largest number in China. Wolong and Jiuzhaigou in Sichuan Province, Changbai Mountain in Jilin Province, Dinghu Mountain in Guangdong Province and Baishui River in Gansu Province have been designated by UNESCO as "World Biosphere Reserves."

Swans, Shandong Province

Environmental Protection 147

Distribution of Major Nature Reserves and Wetlands

- ● National nature reserves
- ● Wetlands

Protecting Endangered Animals and Plants

Volunteers nursing Tibetan antelope calves at Sonam Dargye Protection Station, Hol Xil Nature Reserve

China has rich biodiversity, boasting the world's largest number of bird species and gymnosperm varieties. But China's biodiversity is facing a critical situation: 15 percent to 20 percent of its higher plant varieties are endangered, and over 40 percent of gymnosperm and orchid as well as 233 kinds of vertebrate animals are on the brink of extinction; the numbers of 44 percent of its wild animals are declining, and the population of wild animals not under national protection is decreasing notably.

As one of the earliest signatory countries to the Convention on Biological Diversity, China has been active in international affairs concerning the Convention and vocal on important issues related to biodiversity. It is one of the few countries to have already completed the Convention's action plans.

The Convention demands every signatory country formulate or adjust its national strategies, plans or programs in accordance with its national conditions and in a timely fashion. The China Biological Diversity Protection Action Plan, completed in 1994, provides regulations for eco-environmental protection activities. To date, the seven major targets stipulated in the Action Plan have been basically realized.

In recent years, with the emergence of such issues as genetically modified organisms, alien species invasion, and access to and sharing of biological genetic resources, biodiversity protection is drawing increasing attention from the world community. The general trend of decline in biodiversity in China has not been fully checked, and the situation of biological species resources loss has not been fundamentally changed.

Golden monkey and Chinese yew, both under first-class state protection

Giant panda in Wolong National Nature Reserve, Sichuan Province

To implement the Convention, further strengthen its biodiversity protection, and effectively address new problems and meet new challenges arising in the course of biodiversity protection, China has compiled its Biodiversity Protection Strategy and Action Plan (2011-2030), putting forward overall goals, strategic tasks and priority actions for biodiversity protection in the coming 20 years.

So far, over 400 centers have been established for the raising of wild plant varieties or genetic protection, and artificial breeding of hundreds of wild plants. To help save endangered wildlife, 250 wildlife breeding centers have been established, and special projects have been conducted to protect such endangered species as the giant panda and crested ibis.

In accordance with the Law on the Protection of Wildlife, any criminal act damaging wildlife resources is subject to punishment. The release of the Law has basically reversed the decline of endangered species, and over 70 critically endangered species such as giant panda, crested ibis and Chinese alligator are gradually being freed from the risk of extinction and their habitats are increasingly improving.

ENGOs

The development of China's environmental non-governmental organizations (ENGOs) can be traced back to its first organization – the Chinese Society for Environmental Sciences, established in May 1978 and initiated by the government. Then the Black Beak Gull Protection Association was founded in 1991. In 1994 Friends of Nature was founded in Beijing by Liang Congjie and over 20 environmental protection volunteers. Since then, a number of ENGOs have been founded one after another.

The Green Camp recruited a large number of college students as "green" volunteers, many of whom later became leading environmentalists. Touched by the story of Sonam Dargye, who sacrificed his life to protect Tibetan antelopes from poachers, Yang Xin has devoted himself to the protec-

Pupils and their environment-themed paintings, in celebration of World Earth Day

tion of the Tibetan antelopes and the source of the Yangtze River. Other environmental activists include Liao Xiaoyi who founded the Global Village of Beijing, and Wang Yongchen, a journalist at China National Radio, who founded the Green Earth Volunteers.

Currently, there are about 8,000 ENGOs in China. Among them, the All-China Environment Federation is the biggest and best known, and enjoys government support.

As the Chinese society develops, acute problems such as regional environmental protection and increasing consumption-generated pollution keep emerging, and individual environmentalists are getting involved in various social conflicts, especially environmental ones.

In this regard there has been a long-standing argument over the abuse of hydropower in southwest China, during which the ENGOs started to exercise supervision over social management. They have been striving to air their views on major environmental issues and are keen to take part in decision-making concerning environmental protection in important economic activities. For example, in public environmental protection events such as building trash incinerators at Beijing's Liulitun and introducing maglev suspension train projects in Shanghai, the wide participation of ENGOs stirred nationwide attention and renders them a significant social force.

Liao Xiaoyi, a renowned environmentalist

The ENGOs also combine their efforts for greater influence. The Green Choice Alliance Program was born from this. It was initiated by 21 ENGOs in 2007, including the Institute of Public & Environmental Affairs led by Ma Jun, Friends of Nature, Green Earth Volunteers and Global Village of Beijing. The Green Choice Alliance Program calls on the public not to buy products made by polluting enterprises, thus preventing their products entering the market. As the program expands it is attracting more and more attention among ordinary people by intensifying supervision over polluting enterprises. Inspired by them, some influential media, including China Central Television, have exposed and questioned the conduct of polluting enterprises.

In another case, eight ENGOs in Nanjing united to protect the ecological environment of Purple Mountain in the city's suburb, and the "26℃ Limit for Air-conditioners" activity initiated by Liao Xiaoyi, Wang Yongchen and others in Beijing was finally adopted by the Chinese government as a state policy.

International Cooperation

China actively supports global environmental efforts, and plays a constructive role in international environmental affairs. To date, it has acceded to over 50 international conventions concerning environmental protection, and actively carries out its obligations. The Chinese government has promulgated more than 100 policies and measures on the protection of the ozonosphere and met the gradual reduction goals stipulated in the Montreal Protocol on Substances That Deplete the Ozone Layer.

The China Council for Cooperation on Environment and Development was created as the first body of its kind in the world. It consists of some 40 experts and serves as a senior consultancy for the government. It has made many constructive proposals to the Chinese government, and is regarded overseas as a model of international environmental cooperation.

China actively participates in and promotes regional cooperation on environmental protection, having formed an initial cooperation framework with others, including the China-Japan-Korea Tripartite Environment Ministers Meeting, the China-Europe mechanism for ministerial dialogue on environmental policies, the Asia-Europe Ministers Meeting, environmental cooperation with Arabic states and environmental cooperation mechanisms within the framework of the Shanghai Cooperation Organization.

China maintains good cooperative relations with the UN Environment Program, UN Development Program, Global Environment Facility, World Bank and Asian Development Bank. Bilateral cooperation agreements and memorandums have been signed between China and the US, Japan and Russia. A number of cooperative projects have been implemented under bilateral programs with the EU, Germany and Canada, and international organizations.

The global ENGOs, among them the Worldwide Fund for Nature and the International Fund for Animal Welfare, cooperate with the Chinese authorities and ENGOs, with positive results.

Chinese Minister of Environmental Protection Zhou Shengxian and his US counterpart Gina McCarthy at the 4th Meeting of Sino-US Joint Committee on Environmental Cooperation, December 9, 2013

中　国　C h i n a

China has the world's largest number of people receiving formal education. A multi-level education system involving formal schooling, vocational training and lifelong learning is rapidly becoming complete. The popularization of education drives the advance of science and technology, with over 60 percent of China's science and technology now having reached or nearing the international advanced levels.

Education and Science

- Education System
- Education Planning
- International Exchanges
- Science and Technology
- Innovations in Science and Technology
- International Cooperation
- Social Sciences

Education System

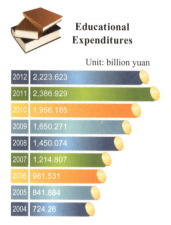

Educational Expenditures

Unit: billion yuan

2012	2,223.623
2011	2,386.929
2010	1,956.185
2009	1,650.271
2008	1,450.074
2007	1,214.807
2006	981.531
2005	841.884
2004	724.26

China implements nine-year compulsory gratis education. Preschool education includes kindergartens and other forms; after compulsory education, education includes standard high schools, secondary specialized schools; and higher education includes junior college and above. Various types of continuing education are also available.

Nine-year compulsory gratis education is the foundation of China's education system. As a populous country, China attaches great importance to basic education. It has implemented compulsory gratis education in both urban and rural areas, with the funds being fully guaranteed by the national exchequer. This is a historic change in China's education system, realizing the centuries-old ideal that "in education there should be no distinction of social status."

Having ensured schooling for almost all children, the government is turning to deal with the unbalanced allocation of

Tsinghua University, Beijing

compulsory educational resources: to give preferential treatment to rural, ethnic minority, border and poverty-stricken areas in allocation of educational resources nationwide or within a province (autonomous region or municipality); and give preferential treatment to disadvantaged schools within a city or county to achieve a balanced allocation of teachers, equipment, books and school buildings. Although the imbalance in compulsory education cannot be redressed immediately due to the great economic and social disparities between different regions, the Chinese government spares no effort to promote educational equality.

Post-compulsory education continues to improve. In order to safeguard the basic right of every citizen to receive further education, the government has initiated effective ways of assistance, including national scholarship, national education-encouragement scholarship, state stipend, student loans, work-study program, college scholarships, financial aids for students from poor families, food allowances and tuition waivers, as well as measures such as preferential registration treatment for first-year students from poor families, and facilities for the state to repay tuitions or student loans for those serving in community organizations or in the armed forces after graduation.

Children and teachers at a kindergarten in Shandong Province

China's Educational Provision Reaching the Average of Middle-income Countries

According to its sixth nationwide population census, China's illiteracy rate had fallen to 4.08 percent. For every 100,000 people, 8,930 had college or postgraduate degrees in 2010, compared with 3,611 in 2000. Net elementary school enrollment was 99.79 percent, and gross enrollment rates in junior and senior high schools, and higher-learning institutions were, respectively, 100 percent, 85 percent and 30 percent. The illiteracy rate in the young and middle-aged population was under 2 percent, and that in the adult population is under 5 percent.

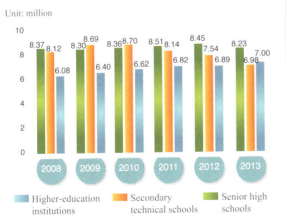

Graduates of Beijing Jiaotong University in their baccalaureate gowns

The national student financial aid system has continued to develop, establishing a comprehensive subsidization system which provides nearly 100 billion yuan every year and has aided a total of 80 million students from preschool to post-graduate education. The free program for secondary vocational education covers all students from rural areas and poor families, and students studying agriculture-related majors.

The schooling of children from special groups is guaranteed. Rapid industrialization and urbanization have brought about large numbers of rural migrant workers. This makes the schooling of their children in populous big cities an increasingly severe and complex problem. The government will further improve the policy for migrant children's schooling, endeavoring to ensure they receive free compulsory education at full-time state schools.

Chinese laws have defined the right to education of people with disabilities. Besides schools for special education, the

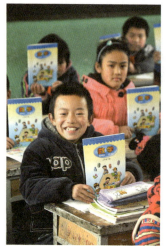

Textbooks are free in primary schools.

Students of Different Types and Levels of Schools in 2013

Graduate colleges for master's degrees
Enrollment 611,000
Number of students 1.794 million
Number of students receiving master's degrees 514,000

Higher-education institutions
Enrollment 6.998 million
Number of students 24.681 million
Number of graduates 6.387 million

Secondary technical schools
Enrollment 6.983 million
Number of students 19.602 million
Number of graduates 6.781 million

Senior high schools
Enrollment 8.227 million
Number of students 24.359 million
Number of graduates 7.99 million

Junior high schools
Enrollment 14.961 million
Number of students 44.401 million
Number of graduates 15.615 million

Primary schools
Enrollment 16.954 million
Number of students 93.605 million
Number of graduates 15.811 million

Special schools
Enrollment 66,000
Number of students 368,000
Number of graduates 51,000

Kindergartens
Number of children 38.947 million

Education System

Higher Education	Postgraduate
	University and College
	Polytechnic and Vocational College
Secondary Education	Secondary Vocational School
	Secondary Technical School
	High School (Junior and Senior)
Primary Education	Primary School
	Kindergarten and Preschool
Adult Education, Military College, Private College, Religious College	
Special Education	
Continuing Education, On-job Education	

Project Hope

"Project Hope" is a public welfare program carried out by the China Youth Development Foundation since 1989. It aims at financing drop-outs in poverty-stricken areas to return to school, establishing elementary schools and improving rural educational conditions. On May 20, 2007 Project Hope shifted from its "rescue" mode toward "rescue plus development," paying more attention to impoverished students' potential for self-improvement.

School supplies donated through Project Hope to students from underprivileged families, Zhejiang Province

disabled children capable of adapting to regular study conditions can enroll in standard elementary and high schools. For this, more special schools are being built, along with efforts to create conditions for them to attend standard schools.

As more than half of the total population and school-age children live in the countryside, rural education is especially important in China. Over the years, rural education has been progressing smoothly. Since 2006 the state has exempted rural students from tuition fees during the compulsory education period, and provided them with free textbooks, which has significantly reduced the rural illiterate population. It also carries out a nutrition improvement program that benefits over 30

Tibetan pupils in class, Tibet Autonomous Region

http://www.moe.gov.cn/
The official website of the Ministry of Education, which regularly releases information and news about China's education. It has an English version.

http://www.jyb.cn/
China Education News Network, an educational information website run by China Education Press Agency.

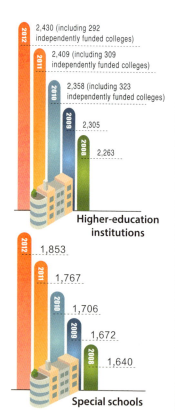

Higher-education institutions
- 2012: 2,430 (including 292 independently funded colleges)
- 2011: 2,409 (including 309 independently funded colleges)
- 2010: 2,358 (including 323 independently funded colleges)
- 2009: 2,305
- 2008: 2,263

Special schools
- 2012: 1,853
- 2011: 1,767
- 2010: 1,706
- 2009: 1,672
- 2008: 1,640

million rural students at the compulsory education stage. In addition, efforts have been intensified to promote the training of rural teachers.

In 2013 China launched an educational poverty-alleviation program, renovating poor schools for compulsory education in rural areas. The nutrition improvement program has been extended to 32 million children. Local governments grant living subsidies to teachers in contiguous poverty-stricken areas. The number of students from poverty-stricken areas admitted by key national colleges was 8.5 percent higher than in 2012.

China's educational horizons are expanding, with the number of candidates for master's degrees and higher continuing to soar. The education market has skyrocketed; and training for computer and foreign-language skills and various professional qualifications are booming. Continuing education is the trend.

Such rapid educational progress is partly attributed to the greatly increased educational investment. The proportion of educational funds in China's financial expenditure has risen by over one percentage point annually since 1998. Following a Ministry of Education program, the Chinese government will set up an educational finance system that matches the public finance system, emphasizing the responsibilities of governments at all levels for funding education, and ensuring faster growth of their financial allocations for education compared to regular revenues.

Education Planning

The Outline of the National Program for Long- and Medium-term Education Reform and Development (2010-2020) is China's first educational plan in the 21st century. It provides guidelines for China's education reform and development. At the present stage, institutional reform is the key to education reform. The Outline focuses on institutional and teaching reforms in elementary, vocational and higher-learning institutions, and teacher training, which together will have a great impact on China's reform of its educational system.

Students and a teacher walking home, Anhui Province

Students learning traditional stone carving techniques under the guidance of their teacher, Chongqing

According to the Outline, China will basically realize education modernization, and become a human resources power by 2020. The Outline sets higher targets for education popularization: to make preschool education basically universal; improve the quality of nine-year compulsory education; popularize senior high school education, with a gross enrolment rate of 90 percent; accelerate the popularization of higher education, with a gross enrolment rate of 40 percent; eliminate illiteracy in the young and middle-aged population; extend the average schooling duration of the incoming labor force from 12.4 years to 13.5 years and that of the working-age population from 9.5 years to 11.2 years, giving 20 percent of the latter higher education and doubling the figure for 2009.

The Outline also emphasizes equal access to education for all. China will establish a basic public education system covering both urban and rural areas, achieve the equalization of basic public education step by step, and narrow the gaps among regions; effectively promote equal access to compulsory education of children of migrant workers; and safeguard the right to education of people with disabilities.

To meet the skyrocketing demand for highly skilled workers, the state is working on two vocational education programs: training personnel urgently needed by the modern manufacturing and service industries, and training rural labor migrating to urban areas.

New Measures Cultivating Competent Students

China is paying more attention to the equitable development of education, and achieving educational progress on an individual basis. The 2014 report on the work of the government underlined the improvement of the competence of every single student in the course of deepening the comprehensive reform of education, including ensuring children's proper nutrition in poverty-stricken rural areas, developing preschool education, implementing the special education promotion scheme and encouraging private schools. All these measures show China's shift of education in the direction of cultivating competent students.

International Exchanges

http://www.csc.edu.cn/

This website, initiated by the non-profit China Scholarship Council directly under the Ministry of Education, provides Chinese students with online information about studying abroad and scholarships. It has an English version.

http://www.cscse.edu.cn/

This website, sponsored by Chinese Service Center for Scholarly Exchanges, provides information relating to studying abroad, Chinese students' return after overseas study, foreign students studying in China, and international exchanges and cooperation in education.

China is seeing active cooperation and exchanges in education with the rest of the world. Exchange students are a major part of this, and no other country has more people studying abroad than China. The number of foreign students studying in China has also increased rapidly. By 2020 the number of overseas students is estimated to reach 500,000, the most among all Asian countries. Overseas student programs have become an important bridge for friendly exchanges between China and the rest of the world.

The introduction of high-quality educational resources is also a trend. China welcomes more world-class experts and scholars to teach, do scientific research and handle management in China, and works to bring in top professionals and academic groups in a planned way. Excellent teaching materials are introduced, and more foreign teachers are teaching in institutions of higher learning. Chinese citizens studying abroad are encouraged to return after finishing their studies.

Today, learning the Chinese language has become popular worldwide. Since 2004 China has worked with other countries and opened not-for-profit Confucius Institutes overseas, with

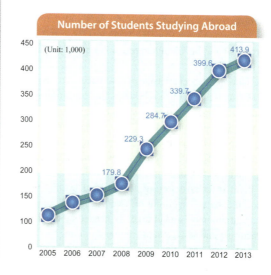

A student from Georgia displaying the brewing techniques of Longjing tea in China National Tea Museum, Hangzhou, Zhejiang Province

the aim of spreading knowledge of the Chinese language and Chinese culture. By the end of 2013 a total of 440 Confucius Institutes and 646 Confucius classrooms had been established in 120 countries and regions.

Science and Technology

A hundred years ago China had no modern science and technology at all – fewer than 10 people in the country understood calculus. But by the early 21st century the hi-tech research and development gap between China and the advanced countries had shrunk visibly; 60 percent of China's technology sector, including atomic energy, space technology, high-energy physics, biosciences, computer and information technology and robotics, have reached or are close to the advanced world levels.

Ocean exploration expedition preparing for an experiment

China's R&D Expenditures

2013	1,190.6 billion yuan
2012	1,029.84 billion yuan
2011	868.7 billion yuan
2010	706.3 billion yuan
2009	580.2 billion yuan
2008	461.6 billion yuan
2007	371 billion yuan
2006	300.3 billion yuan

China's R&D expenditure in 2013 was 1,190.6 billion yuan or 2.09 percent of its GDP, up 15.6 percent year-on-year. A number of innovations have taken place in scientific cutting-edge and strategically important areas. The *Shenzhou-10* manned spacecraft docked with the *Tiangong-1* space station; the *Chang'e-3* spacecraft completed China's first soft landing on the moon and the lunar rover *Yutu* commenced moon explorations; the manned submersible *Jiaolong* went through deep-sea tests for scientific research; the Supercomputer *Tianhe-2* was developed, capable of an Rmax (maximum range) of 54.9PFlops.

Winners of the State Preeminent Science and Technology Award

Year	Winner(s)
2013	Zhang Cunhao (1928- , physical chemist)
	Cheng Kaijia (1918- , nuclear physicist)
2012	Zheng Zhemin (1924- , physicist)
	Wang Xiaomo (1938- , radar engineer)
2011	Xie Jialin (1920- , physicist)
	Wu Liangyong (1922- , architect and urban planner)
2010	Shi Changxu (1920-, material scientist)
	Wang Zhenyi (1924- , haematologist)
2009	Gu Chaohao (1926- , mathematician)
	Sun Jiadong (1929- , rocket and satellite engineer)
2008	Wang Zhongcheng (1925- , neurologist)
	Xu Guangxian (1920- , chemist)
2007	Min Enze (1924- , petrochemical engineer)
	Wu Zhengyi (1919- , botanist)
2006	Li Zhensheng (1931- , plant geneticist and leader of distant hybridization of wheat)
2005	Ye Duzheng (1916- , meteorologist)
	Wu Mengchao (1922- , hepatobiliary surgery scientist and surgeon)
2003	Liu Dongsheng (1917-2008, geologist and environmental scientist)
	Wang Yongzhi (1932- , aerospace scientist)

Innovations in Science and Technology

Pupils from Shaanxi Province attending a space lecture delivered by astronaut Wang Yaping from *Shenzhou-10*

Launch of the *Shenzhou-10* Spacecraft

The manned *Shenzhou-10* spacecraft was successfully launched in June 2013. It was a landmark for China to build a space station, and a further step in China's manned space program. It also marked China's debut in conducting scientific endeavors in space, and prepared for Chinese astronauts' long-term stay in space.

Chang'e-3

Chang'e-3 was the lunar lander for the second phase of the Chinese Lunar Exploration Program, or Chang'e Program, by China National Space Administration (CNSA). *Chang'e-3* was launched in December 2013 atop a Long March 3B rocket from the Xichang Satellite Launch Center in southwest China's Sichuan Province. Carrying China's first lunar rover *Yutu* (*Jade Rabbit*), it completed China's first soft landing on the moon. Later the *Yutu* rover commenced explorations on the moon during its three-month mission.

A child is attracted by the maglev model of *Chang'e-3* at Nanjing Science & Technology Museum

High-speed Rail

By the end of 2013 China had 103,000 km (64,000 miles) of railways, including 11,000 km (6,835 miles) of high-speed rail (HSR), the longest HSR network in the world. The passenger trips by rail during the year saw a year-on-year growth of 10.3 percent, reaching 2.068 billion, topping 2 billion for the first time. The railways also carried 3.22 billion tons of freight. The world's first alpine HSR operating at high latitudes and low temperatures in winter from Harbin to

At a high-speed railway station

Tianhe-2 supercomputer

Dalian was completed and opened to traffic. The Beijing-Shijiazhuang and Shijiazhuang-Wuhan passenger-only railways began operation, completing the Beijing-Guangzhou HSR line – the world's longest. The Hefei-Bengbu HSR, Hankou-Yichang HSR and other key projects were all opened on schedule.

Tianhe-2 Supercomputer

Tianhe-2, the world's first 50-petaflop supercomputer, was developed by China in May 2013. With a peak performance of 54.9PFlops, it is the fastest supercomputer according to the TOP500 list of the world's most powerful supercomputers. Compared with the *Tianhe-1*, which once topped the TOP500 list of fastest supercomputers for November 2010, the *Tianhe-2* is 10 times higher in performance and computing density, and three times higher in energy efficiency ratio.

Super-hybrid Rice Yields 1,000 Kg per *Mu* (c. 0.067 ha) on 7-ha Experimental Lots

Super-hybrid rice yields over 1,000 kg per *mu* (c. 0.067 ha) on 7-ha experiment lots

The fourth-term super rice strain "Y Liangyou 900" by the innovation team of "father of hybrid rice" and CAE academician Yuan Longping set a world record, with highest *mu*-yield of 1,045.9 kg and an average *mu*-yield on a 101.2-*mu* field of 998.1 kg, the Ministry of Agriculture announced in September 2013. Calculated in weighted average or with a 14 percent water content added as allowed by international standards, the yield topped 1,000 kg.

International Cooperation

China has signed inter-governmental scientific and technical cooperation agreements with nearly 100 countries and regions, and joined over 1,000 international scientific and technological cooperation organizations. Such cooperation has also become an increasingly important aspect of China's relations with the US, Russia and the EU.

China and the US have carried out hundreds of joint projects in science and technology, with tens of thousands of scientists and engineers participating. China also enjoys a broad range of fields of cooperation with Russia, especially in aircraft manufacturing, and nuclear power and space technologies. A conference to celebrate China-EU cooperation in aviation R&D was held in Brussels in March 2014, and experts from the two sides discussed future cooperation. In addition, China will continue to enhance cooperation with the US, Germany and Japan in fields such as new energy and environmental protection technologies.

China proactively participates in international technical cooperation projects. It delivered in June 2013 the first batch it developed to International Thermonuclear Experimental Re-

Workshop of a new energy company in Jiangsu Province

Scientist from Chinese National Human Genome Center in Shanghai conducts an experiment.

National Science and Technology Award Conference

The 2013 the National Science and Technology Award Conference was held at the Great Hall of the People in Beijing on January 12, 2014. Eight scientists from the US, Germany, Italy and other countries received the China International Science and Technology Cooperation Award, which is a national-level award established by the State Council for foreign scientists, engineers and management experts or organizations which make great contributions to China's sci-tech progress. Since 1995 a total of 87 foreign experts and one international organization have received the award. They witnessed the maturity of China's international cooperation in science and technology.

National Science and Technology Award Conference

actor (ITER). China is one of the seven members of this international technical project, undertaking the R&D of 10 percent of procurement packages.

With more and more Chinese scientists involved in other multinational technical programs, such as the Beijing electron-positron collider, Human Genome Project, Galileo Project and Daya Bay Reactor Neutrino Experiment, China's increasing participation in international technical cooperation shows that it is eager for more mutually beneficial cooperation.

With the development of its technology and economy, China has taken a more active attitude toward cooperation with others in science and technology, and established more balanced relations with them from simply importation in the past. Chinese participants in those cooperation projects become diversified, with provincial and municipal governments, universities and enterprises holding various sci-tech seminars, exhibitions and investigation activities. The forms of cooperation also deepen, from personnel exchanges and technical transfers to joint R&D of key technologies.

Social Sciences

The Chinese Academy of Social Sciences (CASS) is the premier academic organization and comprehensive research center of China in the fields of philosophy and the social sciences, consisting of 31 research institutes and 45 research centers that cover nearly 300 sub-disciplines, including 120 key sub-disciplines. CASS has more than 4,200 staff members, of whom more than 3,200 are professional researchers, including 1,676 senior and 1,200 intermediate researchers. In addition to a group of experts and scholars of the highest attainments who have international reputations, many middle-aged and young researchers have made noteworthy achievements in theoretical research.

In January 2014 CASS announced the publication of five books, including *History of the Republic of China* (36 volumes), *An Outline History of China* and *A Concise Reading of Chinese History*.

Over the past few years CASS has published a series of "blue papers" on China's current social situation every year, which serve as authoritative references for various industries. Many

CASS institutes serve as official think tanks, offering advice for government policy-making. Annual research reports published by these institutes provide definitive data analyses and experts' opinions for China's social development.

Many universities and colleges in China, like Peking University, Renmin University of China (RUC) and Fudan University, also boast research institutes and experts on social sciences. The second Wu Yuzhang Humanities and Social Sciences Lifetime Achievement Award was presented at the RUC in December 2013. For their outstanding achievements in social sciences, Dai Yi (a noted historian and professor of RUC) and Zhang Zhuoyuan (a leading economist and researcher at CASS) received the award.

Chinese social sciences researchers have attended international academic activities more frequently. Together with other scholars from over 20 countries, Chinese experts participated in the Eighth Forum of the World Association for Political Economy (WAPE) held in Brazil in May 2013. An international symposium dominated by Chinese scholars was held at the United Nations Headquarters in New York in April 2014, with the theme of "Taking Advantage of Innovation: Cultivating National Competitiveness in Innovation to Promote Global Development." With their increasing academic exchanges and cooperation with foreign experts, Chinese social sciences institutes will further expand and deepen their international cooperation and attract the most talented people from all over the world.

Xipo Neolithic site, Sanmenxia, Henan Province

Children attending lectures on "Traditional Chinese Studies" in Changchun Children's Library, Jilin Province

http://cass.cssn.cn/
The official website of Chinese Academy of Social Sciences, publishing information and releasing news about the work of CASS.

http://www.cssn.cn/
Chinese Social Sciences Net, sponsored by CASS and presented by Social Sciences in China Press (SSCP), publishing information about China's social sciences. It has an English version.

中 国 C h i n a

China is a populous country. Measured by the World Bank's poverty line standard, China has lifted 500 million people out of poverty over a period of 20 years, and great changes have taken place in the Chinese people's lives compared to 65 years ago when the PRC was founded.

People's Well-being

- Income and Consumption
- Employment
- Social Security
- Medical Care and Health

Income and Consumption

In 2013 the per capita net income of China's rural residents was 8,896 yuan, growths of 12.4 percent and 9.3 percent after adjusting for inflation, compared to the previous year. The per capita median net income of rural residents was 7,907 yuan, a rise of 12.7 percent. The per capita disposable income of urban residents reached 26,955 yuan, increases of 9.7 percent and 7.0 percent after adjusting for inflation, compared to the previous year. The per capita median income of urban residents was 24,200 yuan, a rise of 10.1 percent.

Household Savings

Unit: billion yuan

Year	Year-end Balance			Annual Increase		
	Total	Time Deposit	Current Deposit	Total	Time Deposit	Current Deposit
1980	39.58	30.49	9.09	11.48	13.85	−2.37
1985	162.26	122.52	39.74	40.79	32.43	8.36
1990	711.96	590.94	121.02	193.51	170.09	23.42
1995	2966.23	2377.83	588.41	814.35	693.96	120.39
2000	6433.24	4614.17	1819.07	471.06	118.66	352.40
2001	7376.24	5143.49	2232.76	943.01	529.32	413.69
2002	8691.07	5878.89	2812.17	1314.82	735.41	579.41
2003	10361.77	6849.87	3511.90	1670.70	970.97	699.73
2004	11955.54	7813.89	4141.65	1593.77	964.02	629.76
2005	14105.10	9226.35	4878.75	2149.56	1412.47	737.09
2006	16158.73	10301.14	5857.59	2054.40	1077.73	976.67
2007	17253.42	10493.45	6759.97	1094.69	192.31	902.38
2008	21788.54	13930.02	7858.52	4535.12	3436.57	1098.55
2009	26077.17	16023.04	10054.13	4288.63	2093.02	2195.61
2010	30330.25	17841.39	12488.86	4253.08	1818.35	2434.73
2011	34363.59			4033.34		
2012	39955.10			5591.51		
2013	44760.16			4805.06		

Note: Since 2011 household savings in RMB have discontinued to be divided into time and current deposits in this table.

Spring Festival celebration in an ancient street

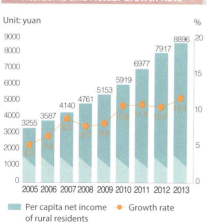

Per Capita Net Income of Rural Residents and Actual Growth Rate

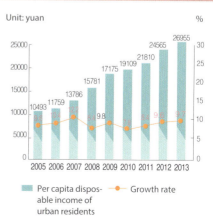

Per Capita Disposable Income of Urban Residents and Actual Growth Rate

Percentages of CPI Changes 2013

Indicator	Nationwide	Urban areas	Rural areas
CPI	2.6	2.6	2.8
Food	4.7	4.6	4.9
Tobacco and liquor	0.3	0.1	0.8
Clothing	2.3	2.2	2.5
Household appliances and maintenance	1.5	1.5	1.3
Healthcare and personal articles	1.3	1.2	1.8
Transportation and communication	-0.4	-0.5	0.1
Recreation, education, and cultural articles and services	1.8	1.7	1.8
Housing	2.8	3.0	2.3

Unit: %

With improving living standards, China's consumption structure has also changed into one allowing extra consumption from simply covering the basic need for food and clothing. The emerging areas of consumption that are expanding at the highest rate include: transportation consumption represented by private cars; communication and information consumption represented by mobile communications; commodity consumption related to housing; and culture consumption represented by education and travel.

In recent years the Chinese government has been paying close attention to the housing market, striving to increase the supply of commercial housing, accelerate the building of low-income housing, and promote the development of public

Abundant supplies

Wedding witnessed by a spring

Unit: million

rental housing, so as to adjust the housing supply structure and provide different types of housing.

China's tourism has boomed thanks to the increased income of its urban and rural residents and more leisure time at their disposal. It is estimated that by 2015 tourism spending will account for 10 percent of China's total household consumption.

All in CARAVANING 2014, Beijing

Employment

> http://www.stats.gov.cn/
>
> As an agency directly under the State Council, the National Bureau of Statistics is in charge of statistics and economic accounting. Its functions include working out regulations on statistical work, formulating directive rules for statistical operations, drawing up plans for statistical modernization and nationwide statistical surveys, organizing and exercising supervision over statistical and economic accounting work in various localities and departments, and supervising and inspecting the enforcement of statistical laws and regulations.

With 9.6 percent of the world's natural resources, 9.4 percent of its capital resources and 1.85 percent of its technological resources, China needs to create jobs for 26 percent of the global labor force – a daunting task for this developing country. In the next four decades China will see further population growth, which will produce large numbers of new workers, unemployed workers and surplus rural labor on a yearly basis.

In its 12th Five-year Plan (2011-2015), China gives top priority to employment for the first time, paying more attention to developing industries and services that are conducive to promoting employment and exploring human resources. During the 12th Five-year Plan period China will create jobs for nine million people each year in urban areas, and control the registered unemployment rate within five percent. Besides, a social security system covering both urban and rural residents will be established by 2020 to include various types of social insurance, subsistence allowance, social relief, charity programs and commercial insurance.

Employment service day

A college graduate at a job fair

After years of efforts a social security framework with Chinese characteristics has been basically established, incorporating basic old-age insurance, basic medical care, unemployment insurance, work-related injury insurance and maternity insurance. The government also provides subsistence allowances to qualified urban and rural residents as part of the social relief system, and is taking robust steps to improve the services.

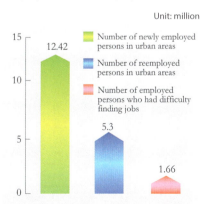

Employment and Reemployment in 2013

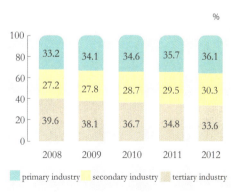

Percentages of Newly Employed Persons in Different Industries in 2008-2012

Social Security

Harmony

China needs to support one fifth of the world's population. This is why its current social security system is only capable of ensuring the basic subsistence needs of its citizens.

The standards are:

◎ Old-age Insurance

Maintenance of a medium standard of living for retirees

◎ Unemployment Insurance

Guaranteeing subsistence for the unemployed

◎ Medical Care Insurance

Providing the insured with basic medical care

Subsistence Allowance Coverage in Urban Areas

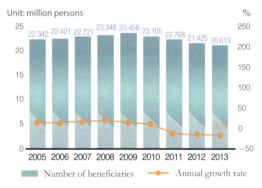

Subsistence Allowance Coverage in Rural Areas

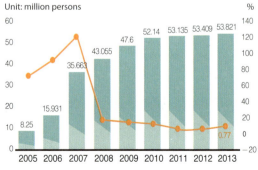

Happy English hours for hearing-impaired children

Medical Care and Health

China introduced its medical care system in the early 1950s to provide medical services to workers either at the expense of the state or as part of labor protection. It is an important component of the country's social security network and a key program of social insurance.

As a form of social insurance, medical care insurance is compulsory and benefits all members of society. The state, therefore, is usually the one to legislate in this regard and implement a medical care system as a compulsory insurance scheme. Funds are raised with contributions from both employers and employees, and the premiums are paid by medical care insurers to reduce medical risks from illnesses or injuries for laborers.

In a nutshell, medical care insurance means that the state or society provides medical services or financial compensation for people who get sick or injured. Now, 99 percent of China's population enjoys basic medical care insurance.

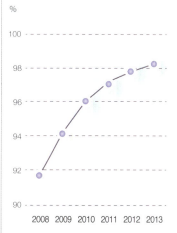

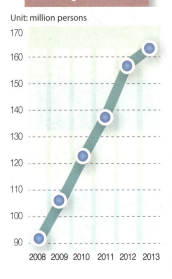

Maternity Insurance Coverage 2008-2013

Unit: million persons

The Chinese people have become healthier. With the average life expectancy reaching 74.83 years in 2010, China has reached the standard of moderately prosperous countries in this regard.

Over the past decade the average life expectancy in China increased from 71.4 years to 74.83 years, growing by 3.43 years, while from 1981 to 2000 it took 20 years to prolong citizens' lives by 3.63 years.

How did this change take place?

Over the past decade China has maintained a 24.4-percent growth rate of its investment in health care, social security and social welfare, far higher than that of the country's GDP growth. With the incremented funds, the Chinese feel much safer about their retirement life and pay less for hospitals and medicines. Senior citizens aged 65 years and above – 80 million

Deng Qiandui, a village doctor from Yunnan Province who went to see patients despite the difficulty in crossing the Nujiang River

Medical Service Contract for Urban Residents

"Improving the rational modes of graded diagnosis and treatment, and establishing a service contract between community doctors and residents" is a highlight in the Decision of the Third Plenary Session of the 18th Central Committee of the Communist Party of China released in November 2013. In China people tend to "swarm" to major hospitals even when they suffer only from minor ailments. If the medical service contract system offers more care to patients, like family doctors do, they will not have to join the crowds at large hospitals. The medical service contract for urban residents is a service agreement signed between community-based medical facilities or general medical practitioners and urban residents. It aims at establishing a relatively stable service contract in which the individual practitioner is responsible for providing medical services for local residents.

People's Well-being 181

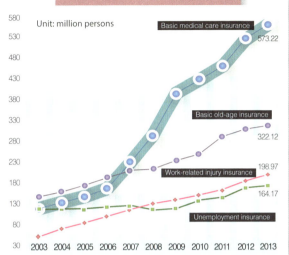

A doctor attends to a patient in the countryside.

in total – can have free health checkups, and the mortality rate of newborns has dropped to 1.31 percent from 2.838 percent in 2000, almost three times faster than the decrease rate in the previous decade.

The average life expectancy of the general world population in 2010 was 69.6 years – 79.8 years in high-income countries and regions and 69.1 years in middle-income countries and areas. Although its average life expectancy is higher than that in the middle-income countries, China still has a long way to go as compared to many other countries and regions.

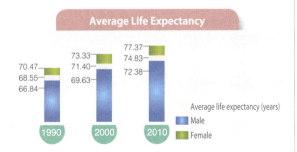

中 国　C　h　i　n　a

Chinese culture refers in general to the culture of the Han Chinese and the culture inherited and created by overseas Chinese, as well as the culture created by China's 55 ethnic-minority groups, including those of the Tibetans, Mongolians, Hui, Zhuang and Miao. Chinese culture is one of the world's oldest, and the only extant and the longest-lasting one among the great civilizations of Egypt, Mesopotamia and India.

Culture and Arts

- Libraries
- Museums
- Preservation of Cultural Relics
- Intangible Cultural Heritage
- Natural and Cultural Heritage
- Literature
- Opera
- *Quyi*
- Music
- Dance
- Calligraphy and Painting
- Cinema
- Mass Media

National Center for the Performing Arts, Beijing

Libraries

Trend of Cultural Development

In 2013 profound changes took place in China's culture industry. For example, the operation of TV program copyright became more mature, the acquisition of mobile game companies increased and the rapid growth of video websites exercised far-reaching influence on program production and dissemination. The Decision of the CPCCC on Some Major Issues Concerning Comprehensively Deepening the Reform raised new requirements for the reform of the culture industry, and highlighted the need to both "increase" and "reduce" something in deepening reform – increasing the dominant role of the market and market competition, and reducing government intervention and companies' reliance on external resources, all of which bear on the diversified development of the culture industry.

China has nearly 3,000 public libraries, with a total collection of over 800 million volumes and copies. Among university libraries, the libraries of Peking and Wuhan universities have the biggest collections. The national library network also comprises libraries of scientific research institutions, various primary-level entities, and elementary and high schools.

With a collection of 31.19 million volumes and copies, and digital resources of 807.3 terabits, the National Library of China is the largest library in Asia. It boasts 730,000 precious documents, of which the number and quality of its ancient tortoise shells carved with Chinese pictographs, documents from the Dunhuang Grottoes, records of different places and scripts of celebrities lead both domestic and overseas libraries. As a general book storehouse of China, it has collected, and continues to collect, most of the books, magazines and newspapers published in contemporary China. It also has the most foreign documents, with a collection of 12.48 million volumes. The library began to accept submissions of domestic official publications in 1916, and domestic electronic publications in 1987. It is China's ISSN (International Standard Serial Number) Center and Library Network Information Center.

The library has formed a digital alliance with other libraries across the country to promote China's digital public information service. It offers access to extensive digital resources of 251 Chinese and foreign-language databases and interactive personalized digital services through new media like comput-

National Library of China, Beijing

ers, digital televisions, cell phones and touchscreen devices. In 2012, more than one million people with disabilities accessed book, lecture and music services from the China Digital Library for the Visually Impaired and the China Digital Library for People with Disabilities. In August 2013 the National Library of China set up an anime databank website where as many as 14,000 types of animation images are available.

The Shanghai Library is China's largest provincial-level library. It has a collection of over 1.7 million volumes of ancient documents, among which there are 25,000 titles of rare books in 178,000 volumes, many being the only surviving copies. The earliest document dates back about 1,500 years.

 Public Cultural Service System

By the end of 2012, radio and television coverage had been extended to all incorporated villages with electricity, and settlements with 20 households and above; 600,000 farmers' libraries had been opened in all accessible incorporated villages; a number of well-equipped museums, art galleries, theaters and concert halls had been completed; all national and provincial art museums had begun to offer free access to the public; all public libraries and cultural centers had started providing free and accessible services to the public. These developments show that the framework of China's public cultural services is already well-formed.

Museums

Over a century has passed since China's first museum, the Nantong Museum, was established by the pioneering entrepreneur Zhang Jian in 1905. The past decade has witnessed rapid development of museums in the country. There are 3,866 museums in China, including 3,219 government-sponsored ones. With a total collection surpassing 23 million items, these museums hold nearly 22,000 exhibitions a year, receiving as many as 560 million visits from spectators annually. Museums based on cultural relics, like the Museum of the Qin Terracotta Warriors and Horses in Xi'an, attract countless visitors from both at home and abroad. The government encourages exchanges of cultural relics between museums, as well as displays and exchanges of legitimate private collections. By 2015 China will have built another 1,000 museums, so that every

Forbidden City, now the Palace Museum, Beijing

city of medium size or larger will possess at least one.

On the east side of Tiananmen Square in Beijing, the National Museum of China covers a floor area of nearly 200,000 sq m. It integrates a variety of functions – archeological findings, collection, research and display, and possesses more than one million items of ancient, modern and contemporary Chinese relics as well as over one million literary documents. The state-of-the-art museum has hosted exhibitions of masterpieces by the world's greatest artists, including Leonardo Da Vinci, Michelangelo and Raphael.

China has entered a private museum era. In this way, owners of private museums allow the public access to private collections. It has been 17 years since the formal registration of Guanfu Museum, the first private museum in China. Currently, private museums number 647, 17.5 percent of the nation's total, and are increasing by about 100 each year. In February 2014 the Private Museums Council was set up, serving as an important platform for the development of China's museums and the dissemination of Chinese culture.

Private museums are following the steps of government-sponsored museums to offer free public admission. To encourage local private museums to open free, the Shanghai Municipal Administration of Cultural Heritage has set up a subsidy as part of a government fund to support their operation.

Preservation of Cultural Relics

China's long-standing civilization has left innumerable cultural relics on its vast territory. World-famous archeological sites include the Peking Man Site at Zhoukoudian near downtown Beijing, Mausoleum of the First Emperor of the Qin Dynasty, Mawangdui Han Dynasty Tomb in Changsha, Mogao Caves in Gansu Province and the underground palace of the Famen Temple in Shaanxi Province.

However, many of China's most precious cultural relics have been removed. Due to reasons such as war and unfair

Fengxian Temple in Longmen Grottoes, Henan Province

> **National Archaeological Site Parks**
>
> National Archaeological Site Parks are models for China to explore ways of major ruins protection. In November 2010 12 archaeological site parks such as Yuanmingyuan and Zhoukoudian were listed as the first batch of national archaeological site parks. In December 2013 another 12 sites including Niuheliang were placed on the list, and 31 more, including Xanadu, were to become national archaeological site parks. So far, there are 24 national archaeological site parks in China.

trade since the First Opium War (1840-1842), more than 10 million items of China's cultural legacy have been lost to Europe, North America, Japan and Southeast Asia. UNESCO estimates that 1.64 million Chinese cultural relics are in the collections of more than 200 museums in 47 countries other than China, and the number of Chinese cultural relics collected by individuals is probably 10 times more than the total collection of museums.

China has nearly 770,000 known permanent sites of historical interest above ground or underground. A total of 4,295 cultural sites are under national protection. A new list of cultural sites, numbering 120,000, under provincial and municipal (county) protection have been approved and released.

The central government's special budget for the preservation of local cultural relics increased by six times from 1.1 billion yuan in 2009 to 7 billion yuan in 2013. In 2013 a total of 14 billion yuan of subsidies were allocated from the central budget, with over 6,000 items of rare and severely damaged cultural relics restored and another 8,000 items of rare cultural relics are to be restored.

Cultural relics have come under increasing legal protection. China has signed all of the four international treaties on relics preservation. The Law on the Protection of Cultural Relics, promulgated in 1982, spells out provisions on immovable cultural relics, archeological excavations, cultural relics preserved in museums and private collections, and the import and export of cultural relics. The Implementation Regulations for the Law on the Protection of Cultural Relics and the Provisional Regulations on the Administration of Relics Auctions were issued in 2003. In 2006 the Measures of Beijing Municipality on the Protection of the Great Wall, the first special regulation of its kind, came into effect.

So far, the government has listed 99 famous historical and cultural cities under state protection, over 80 under provincial-level protection, and 528 historical and cultural towns and villages. An annual 200 million yuan is allocated for their protection.

Traditionally an agricultural country, China has a large number of ancient villages. Their natural environment, as well as folk customs and handicrafts have been well preserved. A large-scale move to protect these ancient villages is being contemplated.

Hongcun, an ancient village in Anhui Province

Craftsman Liu Jie makes a toy figurine with glutinous rice powder, Hubei Province

Carving Chinese characters on woodblock

Intangible Cultural Heritage

China possesses a wealth of intangible cultural heritage. The central government has spent a total of 2.1 billion yuan on the protection of intangible cultural heritage, and in 2013 alone the special funds in this regard exceeded 660 million yuan. In 2006, 2008 and 2011, the State Council released a catalogue of 1,219 state-level intangible cultural heritage items in the 11 categories of folk literature, traditional music, folk dance, traditional opera, quyi, folk art, traditional handicrafts, traditional medicine, folk customs, and competitive sports, games and acrobatics.

On December 4, 2013, UNESCO officially put China's abacus calculation on the UNESCO Representative List of the Intangible Cultural Heritage of Humanity. Till now, a total of 30 Chinese elements, including Kunqu Opera, the art of playing the *guqin* (seven-stringed zither), Uygur Muqam music and Mongolian pastoral songs, have been incorporated in the list. Another seven items such as the Qiang people's New Year Festival and movable-type printing have been incorporated into the List of Intangible Cultural Heritage Items in Need of Urgent Safeguarding. In 2005, for the first time, China submitted a joint application with another country (Mongolia) for Mongolian pastoral songs to be entered on the list.

The Chinese traditional music sound archives, records of the Qing Dynasty Grand Secretariat, list of successful candidates in the Qing Dynasty imperial examinations, ancient records written in Naxi Dongba pictographs

Experiencing pottery making

and the Qing Dynasty architectural design archives of the Lei family have also been inscribed in the Memory of the World program. In 2001 the Tibetan epic *King Gesar*, the world's longest, was listed by UNESCO in its world millennium statements.

China has done a great deal of effective work for the protection of intangible cultural heritage items, including the "China's Folk and Minority Cultures and Arts" series, a compilation of 300 volumes of nearly 500 million words that have preserved numerous rare artistic and cultural resources. In February 2006 the State Council promulgated its Notice on Intensifying the Protection of China's Intangible Cultural Heritage, giving detailed requirements regarding the survey, protection and rescue of intangible cultural heritage items. The Law on Intangible Cultural Heritage, put into effect in 2011, provides legal framework for the protection of China's intangible cultural heritage.

A folk music instruments shop in Kashgar, Xinjiang Uygur Autonomous Region

Natural and Cultural Heritage

China joined the Convention for the Protection of the World Natural and Cultural Heritage in 1985, and began to submit applications in 1986. The Tianshan Mountains in Xinjiang and the Honghe Hani Rice Terraces in Yunnan were listed by UNESCO as World Heritage Sites at the 37th session of the World Heritage Committee held in June 2013. China now has 45 World Heritage Sites, consisting of 31 cultural sites, 10 natural sites and four belonging to both categories.

Since 2004, massive renovations have been made to Beijing's six cultural heritage sites – the Ming Tombs, Great Wall, Forbidden City, Temple of Heaven, Summer Palace and Peking Man Site at Zhoukoudian. Beginning in 2006, China set the second Saturday of every June as Cultural Heritage Day.

The Great Wall
Beijing, 1987, World Cultural Heritage

Imperial Palaces of the Ming and Qing Dynasties
World Cultural Heritage: Forbidden City, Beijing, 1987; Imperial Palace of the Qing Dynasty, Shenyang, Liaoning Province, 2004

Peking Man Site at Zhoukoudian
Beijing, 1987, World Cultural Heritage

Mogao Caves
Gansu Province, 1987, World Cultural Heritage

Mausoleum of the First Qin Emperor
Shaanxi Province, 1987, World Cultural Heritage

Mount Taishan
Shandong Province, 1987, World Cultural and Natural Heritage

Mount Huangshan
Anhui Province, 1990, World Cultural and Natural Heritage

Hall of Supreme Harmony in the Forbidden City, Beijing

Peking Man site at Zhoukoudian, Beijing

CHINA

Mountain Resort and its outlying temples in Chengde, Hebei Province

Ancient buildings in Wudang Mountains, Hubei Province

Classical garden in Suzhou, Jiangsu Province

Summer Palace, Beijing

Jiuzhaigou Valley Scenic and Historic Interest Area
Sichuan Province, 1992, World Natural Heritage

Huanglong Scenic and Historic Interest Area
Sichuan Province, 1992, World Natural Heritage

Wulingyuan Scenic and Historic Interest Area
Hunan Province, 1992, World Natural Heritage

Mountain Resort and Its Outlying Temples, Chengde
Hebei Province, 1994, World Cultural Heritage

Historic Ensemble of the Potala Palace, Lhasa
Tibet Autonomous Region, 1994, World Cultural Heritage

Temple and Cemetery of Confucius and the Kong Family Mansion in Qufu
Shandong Province, 1994, World Cultural Heritage

Ancient Building Complex in the Wudang Mountains
Hubei Province, 1994, World Cultural Heritage

Lushan National Park
Jiangxi Province, 1996, World Cultural Heritage

Mount Emei Scenic Area, Including Leshan Giant Buddha Scenic Area
Sichuan Province, 1996, World Cultural and Natural Heritage

Ancient City of Pingyao
Shanxi Province, 1997, World Cultural Heritage

Classical Gardens of Suzhou
Jiangsu Province, 1997, World Cultural Heritage

Old Town of Lijiang
Yunnan Province, 1997, World Cultural Heritage

Summer Palace, an Imperial Garden in Beijing
Beijing, 1998, World Cultural Heritage

Temple of Heaven, an Imperial Sacrificial Altar in Beijing
Beijing, 1998, World Cultural Heritage

Mount Wuyi
Fujian Province, 1999, World Cultural and Natural Heritage

Dazu Rock Carvings
Chongqing, 1999, World Cultural Heritage

Imperial Tombs of the Ming and Qing Dynasties
World Cultural Heritage: Ming Xianling Mausoleum, Hubei Province, 2000; Qing Dongling Mausoleum and Qing Xiling Mausoleum, Hebei Province, 2000; Ming Tombs, Beijing, 2003; Ming Xiaoling Mausoleum, Jiangsu Province, 2003; three imperial mausoleums of Shengjing, Liaoning Province, 2004

Longmen Grottoes
Henan Province, 2000, World Cultural Heritage

Mount Qingcheng and the Dujiangyan Irrigation System
Sichuan Province, 2000, World Cultural Heritage

Ancient Villages in Southern Anhui – Xidi and Hongcun
Anhui Province, 2000, World Cultural Heritage

Mount Qingcheng, Sichuan Province

Yungang Grottoes, Shanxi Province

Yungang Grottoes
Shanxi Province, 2001, World Cultural Heritage

Three Parallel Rivers of Yunnan Protected Areas
Yunnan Province, 2003, World Natural Heritage

Capital Cities and Tombs of the Ancient Koguryo Kingdom
Liaoning and Jilin provinces, 2004, World Cultural Heritage

Historic Center of Macao
Macao Special Administrative Region, 2005, World Cultural Heritage

Yin Xu
Henan Province, 2006, World Cultural Heritage

Sichuan Giant Panda Sanctuaries
Sichuan Province, 2006, World Natural Heritage

Kaiping *Diaolou* and Villages
Guangdong Province, 2007, World Cultural Heritage

South China Karst Areas
Yunnan and Guizhou provinces and Chongqing Municipality, 2007, World Natural Heritage

Fujian *Tulou*
Fujian Province, 2008, World Cultural Heritage

Mount Sanqingshan National Park
Jiangxi Province, 2008, World Natural Heritage

Mount Wutai
Shanxi Province, 2009, World Cultural Heritage

Historic Monuments of Dengfeng in "The Center of Heaven and Earth"
Henan Province, 2010, World Cultural Heritage

China *Danxia*
World Natural Heritage: Chishui, Guizhou Province; Taining, Fujian Province; Langshan, Hunan Province; Mount Danxia, Guangdong Province; Mount Longhu, Jiangxi Province; Mount Jianglang, Zhejiang Province, 2010

West Lake Cultural Landscape of Hangzhou
Zhejiang Province, 2011, World Cultural Heritage

Site of Xanadu
Inner Mongolia Autonomous Region, 2012, World Cultural Heritage

Chengjiang Fossil Site
Yunnan Province, 2012, World Natural Heritage

Xinjiang Tianshan
Xinjiang Uygur Autonomous Region, 2013, World Natural Heritage

Cultural Landscape of Honghe Hani Rice Terraces
Yunnan Province, 2013, World Cultural Heritage

The Grand Canal
Beijing and Tianjin municipalities, and Hebei, Jiangsu, Zhejiang, Anhui, Shandong and Henan provinces, 2014, World Cultural Heritage

Silk Roads: the Routes Network of Chang'an-Tianshan Corridor
China (Henan, Shaanxi and Gansu provinces, and Xinjiang Uygur Autonomous Region), Kazakhstan (Almaty and Dzhambul provinces), Kyrgyzstan (Chuy Valley), 2014, World Cultural Heritage

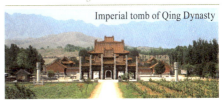

Imperial tomb of Qing Dynasty

Literature

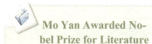

Mo Yan Awarded Nobel Prize for Literature

The Nobel Prize for Literature 2012 was announced to be awarded to Chinese writer Mo Yan on October 11, 2012. Mo began to achieve recognition as a writer in the 1980s for a number of novels and short stories set against the backdrop of rural life in China. He is regarded as one of the *xungen* (root-seeking) writers, who emphasize local cultures. His works are characterized by hallucinatory realism and reveal a paradoxical nostalgia for his hometown in Gaomi County, Shandong Province.

Mo Yan was awarded the Nobel Prize for Literature, December 10, 2012

The Book of Songs, China's first anthology of poems and earliest literary work, was compiled in the 6th century BC. The literature composed in the long succession of dynasties that followed includes pre-Qin (pre-221 BC) prose in a simple style, magnificent Han Dynasty (206 BC-220 AD) *fu* (rhymed prose) and *yuefu* (folk songs). The Tang Dynasty (618-907) alone is credited with thousands of poets, including Li Bai and Du Fu, who together left more than 50,000 poems. The Song Dynasty (960-1279) was known for its *ci* (lyrics), and the Yuan Dynasty (1271-1368) for *zaju* (poetic drama set to music). The Ming (1368-1644) and Qing (1644-1911) dynasties saw the production of four masterpiece novels: *Three Kingdoms, Outlaws of the Marsh, Journey to the West* and *A Dream of Red Mansions*.

Modern Chinese literature has seen two golden ages: the 1920s and 1930s, and the 1980s and 1990s. The first heyday, starting with the New Culture Movement, demonstrated strong opposition to imperialism and feudalism. Progressive writers, exemplified by Lu Xun, pioneered China's modern literature. Lu Xun, Shen Congwen, Ba Jin, Mao Dun, Lao She, Ding Ling and (Eileen) Zhang Ailing have since come to be regarded as modern masters of Chinese literature.

The emergence in the 1980s and 1990s of a number of more internationally influential writers and works reflects the achievements and richness of China's late-20th century literature. Writers showed greater maturity in the use of contemporary language to express the lives and aesthetic experiences of modern Chinese people. Generally speaking, the artistry of thought and literary expression achieved by contemporary novelists surpassed that of the previous generation.

China has dozens of literary awards, the most prestigious of which are the Mao Dun Literary Award, Lu Xun Literary Award, and the annual China Literary Figure of the Year. The Chinese Women's Literary Awards, which are presented every five years, is a major national award scheme covering works by women in the fields of novel, essay, poetry, documentary writing, women's literary theory and translation.

In 1995 China's first literature website, "The Olive Tree,"

was established. The explosion of Internet literature has become the latest eye-catching phenomenon in China's literary world. As a new medium for literature, Internet literature is growing rapidly and greatly influencing the general pattern of Chinese literature as a whole. In 2002 the emergence of www.qidian.com, affiliated to Shanda Interactive Entertainment Ltd, signaled that access to Internet literature was not free any more. In 2007, www.qidian.com launched a bonus plan (100 million yuan to train writers and offer them insurance), the first welfare system ever to fully guarantee and support writers in their artistic creation, greatly promoting the healthy development of original literature.

In 2006 the popularization of the blogosphere stirred up another wave of publication of Internet literature. With more than a decade of development, China's Internet literature has grown from BBS (Bulletin Board System), literary forum and literary website into a huge market with 274 million readers. Internet literature, due to its huge commercial value, has become the industry with the most potential among China's cultural and creative endeavors.

Opera

Chinese traditional opera, Greek drama and Indian Sanskrit opera are considered to be the world's three most ancient opera forms. China boasts more than 300 types of local operas, in-

Peking Opera performance

Peking Opera

Peking Opera is China's representative opera. Over the last 200 years it has developed a repertoire of more than 1,000 works, as well as special sets of musical genres and stylized performance movements. Famous Peking Opera artists, including Mei Lanfang, Cheng Yanqiu, Ma Lianliang and Zhou Xinfang, emerged in the last century, and new artists continue to emerge in the 21st century.

Kunqu Opera

Kunqu Opera has a history of more than 500 years. It is a representative opera of the Ming and Qing dynasties. Listed as one of the Masterpieces of the Oral and Intangible Heritage of Humanity, Kunqu epitomizes the aesthetic beauty of Chinese opera. Kunqu performances feature powerful lyricism, exquisite acting and elegant tunes. The classical repertoire includes *The Peony Pavilion* and *Palace of Eternal Youth.*

A Peking Opera performer puts on makeup.

cluding Peking Opera, Kunqu Opera, Shaoxing Opera, Henan Opera, Cantonese Opera, Sichuan Opera and Shaanxi Opera. Among them, Peking Opera is the most popular and influential. Chinese traditional opera mainly expresses stories through song and dance forms. The Plum Blossom Award is the highest prize for young and middle-aged opera performers.

Modern drama was introduced to China in the early 20th century, and came of age in the 1930s. The Beijing People's Art Theater, founded in 1952, represents the apex of Chinese theater. It has staged nearly 100 dramas, among which *Teahouse* enjoys international prestige as a classical drama. The late Cao Yu is considered one of China's best modern dramatists.

Quyi

Quyi is the name for traditional Chinese spoken and singing arts. It is a unique form of art developed over a long history from oral folk literature and song. There are about 400 *quyi* genres, including comic dialogues, Beijing musical storytelling with drum accompaniment, Yangzhou ditties, Shandong musical storytelling with clappers, Anhui musical storytelling, song-and-dance duets popular in northeast China and Fengyang flower-drum performance. Comic dialogues and storytelling are the most widespread genres, commonly performed on radio, TV and the stage.

Music

As far back as the 1st century BC there were over 80 Chinese musical instruments. Ancient musical works still extant include *Guangling Melody* and *Eighteen Stanzas for the Barbarian Reed Pipe* played on the *guqin* (zither), *Ambush from All Sides* played on the *pipa* (lute) and *Spring Flowers on a Moonlit Night by the River* played by a traditional wind and stringed instrument orchestra.

Since the middle of the 20th century, along with the introduction of Western music and musical instruments, Chinese music has made great progress. Chinese musicians have created a number of outstanding works with national characteristics, including *The East Is Red*, a large-scale music and dance epic; *Red Guards on Honghu Lake*, an opera; and *The Yellow River Concerto*, for piano. Chinese musicians and art performance troupes have participated in a variety of international exchanges and competitions, and won many prizes.

Music festival has become a popular cultural product. The number of music festivals grew from a dozen in 2006 to more than 100 in 2012. Large-scale music festivals are held regularly – for example, the annual Shanghai International Art Festival, Beijing International Music Festival and Beijing International Opera Season. They attract a large number of world-famous musicians and top-level music and art troupes.

National Music Industry Center

Since 2009 a dozen national music industry parks have been set up in four national music industry centers – in Beijing, Shanghai, Guangdong and Chengdu, respectively. The construction of such centers was the first time in the history of China's music industry.

"Esprit Francais" in celebration of the 50th anniversary of the establishment of diplomatic relations between China and France, April 28, 2014, Beijing.

Dance

Performance for the Conference on Interaction and Confidence-Building Measures in Asia, May 20, 2014, Shanghai

Folk Arts and Crafts

China boasts a wide variety of arts and crafts renowned for excellent workmanship. In terms of technique, Chinese folk arts are categorized into cutting, bundling, plaiting, knitting, embroidering, carving, molding and painting. They have strong local flavor and diverse folk styles.

Special arts and crafts involve the use of precious or special materials, combined with elaborate designs and processes to produce works of great elegance. For example, jade carving uses jadestone as its raw material; Jingtai cloisonné enamel gets its name from the Jingtai reign period (1450-1457) of the Ming Dynasty, from blue glaze on copper filament, which after polishing reveals magnificence in design and color.

Chinese folk dancing has a long history, with the country's 56 ethnic groups creating many dances with unique characteristics, such as the northern Han people's *yangge* dance, south China's tea-picking lantern dance, the Mongolian *andai* dance and the Tibetan *xuanzi* dance.

In 1959 the National Ballet of China was founded, introducing Western ballet to China. Ballets with Chinese characteristics, such as *The Red Detachment of Women*, *The Whitehaired Girl* and *Raise the Red Lantern*, enjoy wide popularity. During festivals, folk dancing is a popular form of entertainment; while national song and dance troupes, such as China Opera and Ballet Theater, China Oriental Song and Dance Troupe, China National Ethnic Song and Dance Ensemble and National Ballet of China, present professional, high-standard performances.

Calligraphy and Painting

Chinese written characters are square-shaped, with an emphasis on vigor of style and structure. The art of calligraphy developed naturally from China's unique writing system. Every dynasty had its great calligraphers whose styles came to represent their times, and the Chinese people's love of calligraphy is still fresh today.

Different from Western oil painting, traditional Chinese painting is characterized by unique forms of expression. Its roots can be traced back to paintings on Neolithic pottery 6,000 to 7,000 years ago. Since similar tools were used to draw lines for the earliest painting and writing, painting and calligraphy are said to share the same origin. Chinese paintings often include poems and/or calligraphy. They also often bear the seals of their various owners. Thus the four art forms are integrated, providing a richer aesthetic experience. Figure, landscape, and flower-and-bird paintings are the major traditional painting genres, with masterpieces of different genres emerging in dif-

Preface to the Poems Composed at the Orchid Pavilion, a great Chinese calligraphy work

ferent dynasties.

Contemporary painting and calligraphy are flourishing too. The National Art Museum of China and similar bodies hold individual or joint exhibitions every year, and many exhibitions of traditional Chinese painting have been held overseas. Chinese artists have also made remarkable progress in Western-style oil painting, woodcuts and watercolors, and many have created works that combine traditional Chinese and Western techniques, adding brilliance to both forms. With various kinds of modern materials, forms, frameworks and genres, excellent modern artworks continue to emerge. New media artworks, including video, digital, animated and audio art, are commonly seen at domestic and overseas exhibitions.

Interior of the 798 Art Zone, Beijing

 Modern Art Zones

M50 and 798 are typical modern art zones in Shanghai and Beijing. M50 gets the name from its address at 50 Moganshan Road, Shanghai, and is a gathering-place for many artists from around the world. Situated in the northeast suburbs of Beijing, the 798 Art Zone was previously the site of state-owned electronics factories, including the biggest factory numbered "798." In 2002 groups of artists and cultural organizations began to move in, turning the area into a complex for galleries, art centers, artists' studios, design companies, cafes and restaurants.

Gallery, Shanghai

Cinema

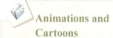

Animations and Cartoons

China's 279 million minors are the consumer group with the most potential for the animation and cartoon industry, a market which is worth over 100 billion yuan every year. In 2004 nine national centers for animation and cartoon works and four teaching and research centers for animation training were established. Since then the animation and cartoon industry has seen an annual growth of over 20 percent in added value. Now China has 20 national centers for animation and cartoon works, and the China International Cartoon and Animation Festival has been held annually since 2005.

China has become the world's third-largest movie producer and No.1 TV drama producer. Its movie box-office sales had grown to 21.769 billion yuan in 2013 from less than 1 billion in 2003. The top 50 box-office movies all exceeded 100 million yuan in ticket sales, with domestic movies taking up 58.65 percent of the total, changing the pattern in which imported movies dominated the Chinese movie market. Within 82 days in 2014, the domestic box-office takings hit 6.3 billion yuan, more than the total box-office takings of 2009, which stood at 6.206 billion yuan.

Realism has remained the mainstream of Chinese cinema. In the wave of filmmaking that rose in the mid-1980s, realistic works reached high levels of creativity in varied subject matters, styles and forms, and in the exploration and innovation of cinematic language. Chinese directors, including Zhang Yimou, Chen Kaige and Huang Jianxin, rose to fame during this period, becoming international cinema celebrities. The late 1990s saw the emergence of directors like Jia Zhangke, Wang Xiaoshuai, Zhang Yuan and Lou Ye, who were mostly born in the 1960s and 1970s. Their movies portray ordinary people's lives in a realistic fashion.

The Changchun and Shanghai international film festivals are annual events. The Golden Rooster is the top prize for Chinese movies. The government has established the Huabiao Awards especially to encourage the mainstream movies. The Hundred Flowers Awards are presented on the basis of audience votes. Other awards also contribute to the development of China's movies, including the Golden Calf Awards for Children's Movies, Hong Kong Film Awards, Golden Bauhinia Awards, Taiwan Golden Horse Awards and Chinese Movie Media Awards.

Mass Media

Online Media

The population of netizens in China has reached 618 million, including 500 million cell phone netizens, as Internet service now covers all towns and townships, and 91 percent

Live telecast of an interview by China Economic Net

of incorporated villages. All towns and townships have broadband access, and commercialization of 4G is in full swing. In 2012 TD-LTE-Advanced, in which China has the leading edge, was established as one of the two international standards for 4G technology, tremendously boosting the speed of mobile communications. It has rapidly spread worldwide.

Since the Ministry of Industry and Information Technology started to formally issue 4G network licenses in December 2013 to China Mobile, China Unicom and China Telecom, China's 4G network development has been put onto the fast track. Before the launch of 4G services, China Mobile had built about 200,000 base stations. By the end of 2014 the 4G network will cover over 300 cities and have over 30 million subscribers.

As the use of the Internet is booming in China, every citizen can be connected to be part of a network. The online media provides the most convenient platform for enlarging information sources and increasing transparency in society.

Since the mid-1990s China's traditional media has joined hands with online media and developed their businesses online. Popular news websites are playing a unique role in news dissemination.

After China Mobile launched its cell-phone TV service in

Crackdown on Online Rumors

"A lie can travel halfway around the world while the truth is still putting on its shoes." This is a description of what has happened in the cyber world. Since August 2013 measures to crack down on online rumors have come to the public's attention. In this campaign, the antics of Qin Huohuo (screen name), Li'er Chaisi (screen name), Xue Manzi and Zhou Lubao beyond the Internet were disclosed.

Mobile reading

By December 2013 China's mobile phone Internet users had reached 500 million, with an annual growth rate of 19.1 percent. In 2013 73.3 percent of the new netizens surfed the Internet via mobile phones, which means that the mobile phone is the most popular Internet terminal and the major impetus of China's netizen growth.

With the boom in the mobile Internet, fast-paced life, fragmented reading and popularization of smartphones, mobile reading such as mobile phone newspapers, magazines and e-books are gradually becoming part of the Chinese people's life.

The e-reader stand of China Telecom at Beijing International Book Fair

http://weibo.com/bjfbt

This was the first provincial-level microblog account, launched in Beijing in November 2011, to release government information.

2005, news images and text became available on cell phones, prompting a spate of news websites to also provide cell-phone reports. In April 2012 Anhui Electronic Audio-Visual Press was officially renamed Time Publishing and Media Co., Ltd. It was the first electronic audio-visual press in China to undertake the strategic transformation into a new media publishing house.

The latest trend in China's media industry is to form transmedia and transregional media operating on multiple patterns. In 2001 the government set a goal of establishing transregional multimedia news groups, and instituted detailed regulations on fund-raising, foreign cooperation and transmedia expansion to this end. The China Radio, Film and TV Group, founded in late 2001, is now China's largest and most powerful multimedia group, covering television, the Internet, publishing and advertising, through integrating the resources of national radio, TV and film organizations, along with those of Internet firms. CCTV's English channel reaches US audiences via News Group's Fox News network.

Online Governance Consultation

With its increasing popularization, the Internet is becoming a major channel for Chinese citizens to exercise their right to know, to participate, to express and to supervise. On June 20, 2008, President Hu Jintao held an online conversation with netizens through www.people.com.cn. Civil servants communicate with the people via the Internet on government policies, making government information more transparent and accessible. Since the micro blog came into being in 2009, it has become the third information source on the Internet following the news and forums. The Internet is of great importance to China's development and crisis management strategy during its period of transformation.

Newspapers

The total and daily circulation of China's daily newspapers have taken the leading positions in the world, with a total circulation of nearly 50 billion copies and average circulation per day over 100 million copies. Newspapers feature diversified forms to cater to different reader groups. The *Shiyan Evening*

News published its 3D edition on April 16, 2010, becoming the first 3D newspaper in China.

Recent years have seen a trend of reorganization of newspapers. So far, nearly 50 newspaper groups have been established, including Beijing Daily Group, Wenhui-Xinmin United Press Group and Guangzhou Daily Press Group. In 2006 Tianjin Daily News Group adopted digital technology in its distribution and, via satellite transmission, began serving immediate-printing and real-time reading of its *Tianjin Daily* in 39 countries.

The influence and competitiveness of newspapers are weakening in the face of the growing popularity of radio, television and the Internet. To compete with the electronic media, the newspaper world is shifting from sole news function to opinion and service functions, providing online and cell phone newspapers while keeping the traditional form. With an electric layout via mobile reading terminals like iPad, the newspapers can continue their traditional procedures of interviewing and editing, layout and business coverage.

Radio

China National Radio, China's official radio station, has 16 channels broadcasting more than 300 hours of programs per day via satellite. Every province, autonomous region and municipality also has its own radio station.

China Radio International (CRI) is the only state radio station targeting overseas audiences. It has 3,200 hours of programs beamed daily across the globe in 51 foreign languages, in addition to standard Chinese (Putonghua), four Chinese dialects and five Chinese ethnic-minority languages.

Television

China's television industry has a complete system of program production, transmission and coverage. China Central Television (CCTV), the state station, now has 42 TV channels, including 30 public channels and 12 digital pay channels, broadcasting a total of 452 programs. In 2012 the total broadcast duration was 341,400 hours, with 935 hours each day to 700 million listeners on the mainland. CCTV is the only TV station in the world to broadcast every day in six working

Mobile Communication through WeChat

The emergence of smartphones has led to a fragmentation of social life. WeChat, first released on the Chinese mainland in January 2011, is currently one of the most popular communication applications for smartphones. In a little more than one year, by the end of March 2012, the population of WeChat users had topped 100 million. The figure doubled in the next six months. In 2013, WeChat users topped 600 million and active users each month reached 355 million.

WeChat also offers such services as taxi booking, hotel reservation and restaurant searches. It is becoming a fixture of daily life at an astonishing pace. In January 2014 Beijingfabu, the first e-governance platform in the country, was launched on both WeChat and microblog, which made WeChat a new platform of communication between the government and the people.

Live broadcast of major conferences in various ethnic minorities' languages

An Uygur TV program editor from Xinjiang TV Station

languages of the UN. It now broadcasts to 171 countries and regions, with a total of 314 million overseas subscribers. In China every province, autonomous region and municipality has its own TV station.

Large international expositions, including Shanghai TV Festival, Beijing International TV Week, China Radio and TV Expo and Sichuan TV Festival, are held on a regular basis. Besides judging entries and conferring awards, these festivals conduct academic exchanges, and import and export TV programs.

China Network Television (CNTV) started broadcasting on December 28, 2009. CNTV has 450,000 hours of videos and assembles programs totaling over 1,000 hours daily from TV stations nationwide. It has done pioneering work in the field of digital preservation of historical and cultural items. It has also established China's largest and most influential multimedia database of copyrighted online videos.

China Xinhua News Network Corporation (CNC) is a television station sponsored by Xinhua News Agency. Its Chinese- and English-language channels broadcast news programs 24 hours a day, covering world news ranging from emergencies to important political, economic and cultural events. As a new international TV agency, CNC broadcasts programs to the Asia-Pacific area, North America, Europe, the Middle East and Africa through satellite, cable, cell phone and the Internet.

Transformation of Cultural Institutions into Enterprises

In the past few years, the for-profit institutions in the publishing, distribution, and film and television industries have completed their transformation into commercial enterprises. Reform and innovation in the cultural sector will continue. In October 2011 the government took important steps to promote the reform of the cultural sector and make cultural industry a pillar of the national economy.

The Third Plenary Session of the 18th CPC Central Committee states that China will continue to transform state-owned for-profit cultural institutions into business enterprises, and adopt for them corporate systems or shareholding systems at a faster pace. China will promote cross-region, cross-sector and cross-ownership mergers and acquisitions of cultural enterprises, so as to make the culture industry larger, more intensive and more specialized.

Publishing

Since the introduction of the reform and opening up policy 30 years ago, China has witnessed a transformation from a "book desert" to a "book ocean," and the mushrooming of millions of publications, and the mode of communication has changed from paper media alone to multimedia.

The number of books and magazines published in China leads the world, with a total of 7.92 billion copies of 410,000 titles of books – up from 12,900 titles in 1977 – and 3.35 billion copies of 9,867 magazines. In the most comprehensive survey of ancient books since the founding of New China in 1949, which was launched in 2007 and completed in 2014, it is estimated that the *Catalogue of Ancient Chinese Books* includes more than 200,000 titles in over 450,000 versions of extant ancient copies dating from before 1912, giving us a clear picture of the cultural legacy of ancient writings.

More than 120 press and publishing groups have been established across the country, with 49 listed on the stock market. In 2012 the total output of the press and publishing industry grew to 1.6 trillion yuan-worth from less than 300 billion yuan-worth a decade ago; 58 provincial/municipal printing organizations received an investment of 21 billion yuan and generated an output value of 21.7 billion yuan; the nine national digital publishing bases have developed rapidly and yielded remarkable results. It is estimated that the sales amount of digital publications will account for 50 percent of the total of China's publishing industry by 2020, and 90 percent of Chinese books will have online counterparts by 2030.

In 2006 the Information Office of the State Council, together with the General Administration of Press and Publications, started "China Book International." In 2009 the Information Office announced more financial support for publishers around the world for translating and publishing books on China for the international market.

In line with China's WTO commitments, the General Administration of Press and Publications in May 2003 promulgated its Administrative Measures for Foreign-invested Book, Newspaper and Periodical Distribution Enterprises, allowing foreign investors to engage in publication retailing as of May 1, 2003, and wholesaling from December 1, 2004. But the Administration's approval is required for any such retail or wholesale organization to be set up.

State Administration of Press, Publications, Radio, Film and Television

On March 22, 2013, the General Administration of Press and Publications and the State Administration of Radio, Film, and Television were merged into a new organ, the State Administration of Press, Publications, Radio, Film and Television.

Under its administration are six industries: book publishing, newspapers, periodicals, radio, television and film – all traditional mainstream media – and some Internet businesses.

http://www.gapp.gov.cn/

Pavilion of Future at the World Expo, Shanghai

中 国　C h i n a

Globalization of fashion has had a full impact upon the life of the Chinese people. Whether in dress, recreation, physical fitness or travel, the Chinese people have taken a global perspective to express themselves. There are many festivals in China. The customs at each festival are different, and constitute important elements of Chinese culture.

Modern Life

- Fad
- Sports and Fitness
- Pastimes
- Travel
- Family Life
- Traditional Festivals

Fad

Shanghai Fashion Week

A 6.5-m-long business suit in Taiyuan, Shanxi Province

A new dress which made its debut at the Cannes Film Festival red carpet show yesterday is seen today at an awards ceremony in China; beer and fried chicken favored by the heroine in a popular South Korean TV drama becomes a fad dish in China overnight; while young American parkour lovers are crazy about their sports, a wing-outfit flight contest is being held in Zhangjiajie, China. Looking at the fashionable men and women on the street of Beijing, one may find that there is no difference between them and those on the streets of Paris, fashion capital of the world, except for skin color.

With the convenience and frequency of communication between China and the rest of the world, China's street fashions synchronize with the world trend. When fashion shows are held during Milan's Fashion Week, the photos of their latest designs find their way to China's fashion magazines. Only one week later, they are seen in the luxury stores of major Chinese cities. More and more foreign fashion models are coming to China, with the details of their schedules revealed in local fashion media. For ordinary Chinese, dressing up with distinctive character is becoming a part of life. On the streets you can see both fashionable sexy girls and punks, and women either in traditional Chinese cheongsams or long floral skirts. People of different professions dress accordingly with distinctive personal traits – the white collars in ironed shirts and ties walking through offices, businessmen in neat suits flying between cities. Chinese cities have become tournament grounds of fashion.

While pursuing fashion, the Chinese are also leading the trend. At the Oscars red carpet show, the Chinese stars in Chinese-style dresses will always be the focus, and even super European and American stars will add oriental elements to express their pursuit of fashion. The Chinese elements have blended into the world and become an inseparable part of fashion circles.

Female students of the 142-year-old True Light High School wear traditional shoes to match their traditional *qipao*, Guangzhou, Guangdong Province

Blend of Chinese and Western Pop Culture

Today more and more entertainment stars worldwide are holding concerts and launching events in China, cultivating a large group of Chinese fans. In 2014 Avril Lavigne held concerts in eight Chinese cities, a tour by the Rolling Stones kicked off in Shanghai, and superstars like Johnny Depp and Brad Pitt came to China to meet their fans and promote their new movies. The South Korean star Lee Min Ho even performed at China's Spring Festival Gala, and is said to have more fans in China than in his home country.

The Rolling Stones concert, March 12, 2014, Shanghai

Traditional Chinese elements become highlights.

Sports and Fitness

Li Na, Australian Open champion, January 2014

In the past, when we talked about Chinese sports, it was always about table tennis. Today, the "small ball era" has come to an end. From swimming to track and field, from tennis to basketball, the names of Chinese athletes are now on the list of the world's top athletes. In early 2014 Chinese tennis player Li Na took the Australian Open title, the second time for her to win a world championship.

Ordinary Chinese people are more interested in sports than ever. Urban residents favor running, and in 2014 marathons in Beijing, Hong Kong and Xiamen attracted about 80,000 participants each. More and more young people are working out in gyms, while middle-aged and elderly people prefer to exercise or jog in the fitness areas of their community. Community dancing has become a fad among middle-aged women. On sunny days you will see people doing traditional sports like shadow boxing, flying kites, kicking shuttlecocks, running, roller skating, practicing hip hop and singing in parks or public squares.

Even in remote towns, sports are also very popular. In Huili, Sichuan Province, a boxing team organized in the 1980s has won over 100 medals, and trained hundreds of excellent boxers. Their story was made into a documentary by a Canadian

http://www.sport.gov.cn/
The official site of the General Administration of Sports of China is responsible for the release of official information on China's sports.

http://www.olympic.cn/
The official site of the Chinese Olympic Committee is responsible for the release of information on the Chinese Olympic Committee, with an English version.

http://www.sport.org.cn/
The official site of the All-China Sports Federation releases information on sports. The Federation is a national non-governmental, non-profit sports organization.

Exercising on public fitness equipment, Chongqing

Students playing with balls at a PE course, September 3, 2012, Nanjing, Jiangsu Province

director and released across the country. Martial arts and sports classes of all kinds are springing up, training backups for the future of China's sports.

The government attaches great importance to developing national fitness programs. Currently, gyms and swimming pools are being built in major cities and opened to the public, basketball courts, table tennis rooms and fitness areas are being built in local communities all over the country. The development of China's sports undertakings has helped to markedly improve the physical fitness of the people. According to a World Health Organization report, the average life expectancy of the Chinese people in 2011 was 76, higher than in other countries at a similar stage of development and even higher than in some European countries. With the improvement of people's living standard, physical fitness is increasingly becoming an inseparable part of the Chinese people's life.

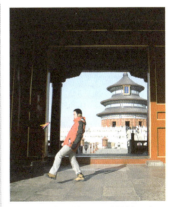

Practicing the old sport of kicking shuttlecock in front of the Hall of Prayer for Good Harvests in the Temple of Heaven, Beijing

Pastimes

Foreign artists invited to perform in Shanghai

Mahjong was once one of the most popular pastimes for the Chinese people, but now it is being joined by a growing variety of recreational activities. Reading is gradually becoming the most popular way of entertainment. Each weekend, libraries in major cities are crowded with readers. Watching movies, going to concerts and watching dramas have also become popular. There are concert halls and theaters in most cities in China, featuring performance troupes from all over the world, and the tickets are always in short supply.

When evening comes, some young people enjoy reading in coffee shops or watching dramas in theaters while others patronize KTVs and bars. As the favored entertainment venues of fashionable men and women, KTVs and bars are found in every city in China. For example, Sanlitun in Beijing, Lan Kwai Fong in Hong Kong, Xuhui District in Shanghai and Lijiang in Yunnan are landmarks of urban night life in modern China. They add color to the infinite vitality of those cities.

Watching TV and surfing on social networks are popular for stay-at-homes. In recent years, China's entertainment programs have been booming, particularly singing competi-

Lan Kwai Fong at night, Hong Kong

Ice sculpture, Harbin, Heilongjiang Province

Outing by bike during the spring, April 8, 2013, Anhui Province

tions. Popular social network services such as microblog and WeChat have become important tools of communication and entertainment for many Chinese people. Mobile games have also become a new trend among young urbanites, who play them on buses, subways, at home and in the office. More than a communications tool, cell phones are also an important recreational tool for young Chinese.

Today the Chinese are embracing more diverse and multiple recreational activities. In spring, they go to the suburbs to play Counter Strike games and fly model airplanes; in summer, they go to amusement parks; in autumn, they go on picnics and ride horses; and in winter they go skiing and enjoy ice lantern festivals. Chinese urban life is colorful nowadays, and everyone can find what he/she likes.

Tremendous Changes in Rural Recreation

Rural recreational activities are no longer limited to chatting, watching TV and playing mahjong. In recent years, the government has built libraries in rural areas across the country to encourage farmers to read during the slack season. Many farmers perform on TV and realize their dream to be a singer. Some farmers even buy components and parts online to make airplane and submarine models on their own threshing grounds during the slack season.

Travel

Today the Chinese people can take one third of a year off from work to travel and visit their families, which are the top choices of most people.

As cars have gradually come into the Chinese people's life, self-driving has become a new travel fad. On holidays and weekends, self-drivers gather through the Internet and make travel plans to enjoy the beauty of Nature. Some wealthy Chinese even have motor homes which are more suitable for long journeys. And traveling around the world is no longer a dream.

More and more average people choose to travel abroad. Besides Southeast Asian countries neighboring China, their destinations also include Europe and America. According to the National Tourism Administration, China's outbound visits numbered about 98 million in 2013 and are expected to sur-

Pasture in Altay, Xinjiang Uygur Autonomous Region

pass 100 million in 2014. Young people are the bulk of these tourists. Most of them are well-educated pursuers of high-quality life, and they prefer to arrange their own travel schedules by booking hotels and air tickets online before leaving.

Hiking is also becoming popular with the young people. On some well-known Chinese hiking websites, many travelers discuss travel plans on weekends. In some cases, dozens or even hundreds of them gather to carry out their two-or-three-day hiking plans together. Wearing outdoor jackets, carrying trekking poles and other gear, these travelers explore the outdoors.

With urbanization, visiting one's family is becoming an important way to spend holidays. Currently, many people living in big cities are from other provinces, and kinship is still something the Chinese hold dear, so on every occasion they will return to their hometowns to visit their parents, relatives and friends no matter how long the journey is. Each Spring Festival, China witnesses the largest-scale migration ever seen in history as millions of people leave the big cities for their hometowns at this time. And after the Festival they will return to the big cities.

1	2	4
	3	

1 Canyoning at Wanquan River, October 2, 2012, Hainan Province

2 Whitewater kayaking, June 13, 2012, Chongqing

3 Many migrant workers bring their children, after a short Spring Festival reunion at their rural homes, back to the metropolis where they work.

4 It's wonderful to return home during the Spring Festival in spite of extremely heavy traffic, Xi'an, Shaanxi Province, January 29, 2014.

CHINA

Badaling section of the Great Wall, Beijing

Average Spending on Domestic Trips

Unit: yuan

2012
- 914.5 | 491.0 | 5.05%
- 767.9

2011
- 877.8 | 471.4 | 22.1%
- 731.0

2010
- 883.0 | 306.0 | 11.7%
- 598.2

2009
- 801.1 | 295.3 | 4.8%
- 535.4

2008
- 849.4 | 275.3 | 5.9%
- 511.0

- National average
- Growth year on year
- Urban tourists' average spending
- Rural tourists' average spending

http://www.qunar.com/

As the largest Chinese travel platform, qunar offers detailed information about air tickets, hotel booking, vacationing, group tourism purchases, etc., for both domestic and overseas travels to help travelers find the most cost-effective product.

http://www.qyer.com/

Created by an overseas Chinese student to share travel information, qyer aims to encourage and help Chinese travelers experience the world through his/her own perspective. Now it has become a platform with millions of travelers sharing information on overseas journeys.

http://www.tuniu.com/

With "making travel easier" as its slogan, tuniu provides travel products covering package, DIY, self-driving and cruise tours, hotel booking, visa application, purchase of scenic spot tickets and corporate travel.

Major Tourism Routes

Essential China Tour
Beijing, Shaanxi, Shanghai and Guangdong.

Great Wall Tour
From Beijing and Hebei to Ningxia and Gansu, visiting the better-preserved sections of the Great Wall.

Sea/Lake Holiday Tour
Twelve national tourism areas, including Sanya in Hainan, Qingdao in Shandong, Dalian in Liaoning, Beihai in Guangxi, Putian and Mount Wuyi in Fujian, and Dianchi Lake in Kunming.

Silk Road Tour
Urumqi, Xining, Yinchuan, Lanzhou and Xi'an, along the ancient Silk Road.

China Health and Fitness Tour
Shanghai, Jiangsu, Hebei and Shaanxi, experiencing traditional Chinese acupuncture and massage, and learning t'ai chi ch'uan and fitness *qigong*.

Religious Culture Tour
Mainly visiting renowned temples or monasteries in Beijing, Shanxi, Anhui, Zhejiang, Sichuan, Hubei, Qinghai and Tibet.

Central China Folk Customs Tour
Shanxi, Henan and Shandong, highlights of folk villages and scenic sites.

Ice and Snow Tour
Liaoning, Heilongjiang and Jilin, to appreciate the rime, ice lanterns and sculptures, as well as folk customs, and skiing.

Southwest China Folk Customs Tour
Yunnan, Guizhou, Guangxi and Sichuan, highlighting minority folk customs, villages and scenic sites.

South China Riverside Village Tour
Hangzhou, Jiaxing and Shaoxing in Zhejiang Province, and Nanjing, Yangzhou, Wuxi and Suzhou in Jiangsu Province, experiencing local landscapes and customs.

Three Gorges Tour
Along the Yangtze River to Chongqing, Sichuan, Hunan and Hubei, visiting renowned natural and cultural sites in the Three Gorges region.

Folk Customs Tour
Along the Yellow River to Qinghai, Gansu, Ningxia, Shanxi, Inner Mongolia, Henan and Shandong, visiting renowned natural and cultural sites.

Landscape Tour
Fujian, Guangxi, Anhui, Guizhou, Hunan, Jilin and Sichuan, visiting renowned natural and cultural sites.

Watchtower of the Forbidden City at sunset, Beijing

Beach in Sanya, Hainan Province

Rime, Jilin Province

The water town of Zhouzhuang, Jiangsu Province

Sunrise at Zhangjiajie, Hunan Province

The Wide Turn on the Yellow River, Shanxi Province

Family Life

An old street in Lijiang ancient town, Yunnan Province

The family is the center of the Chinese people's life, and the home is the basis of their family life. By 2014 the per capita living space of the Chinese people has markedly increased, but with soaring housing prices most young people are still working hard to buy a cozy house. Many people no longer choose to live in downtown areas but prefer houses in the suburbs with a better environment and affordable prices. Some wealthy Chinese prefer to buy free-standing villas with a garden and terrace in the suburbs. Chinese people now have higher standard of housing conditions.

In daily life, health and environmental protection are becoming popular topics. In home decoration, people care more about whether decoration is harmful to health. In transportation, more people choose to cycle or walk to work, as energy conservation has become a popular consensus. Air pollution has become a hot topic and many families are buying air purifiers. In the meantime, food safety has become a concern, and more and more people are choosing organic food. In the suburbs, small farms growing organic food are springing up, sending fresh organic vegetables and fruits to markets every day.

Online shopping has become an important part of everyday life. You can buy almost everything from the Internet such as air-conditioners, washing machines, and even needles and salt with only a click. On the same day or only a few days later, you will receive your purchase at your door. This has brought tremendous changes to people's life.

But people still frequent shopping malls, as finding or trying clothes and other goods in entity shops is quite different from shopping online. So the downtown areas of Chinese cities are full of people and business opportunities.

Shoppers buying organic food in a supermarket on April 5, 2014 in Xuchang, Henan Province

Traditional Festivals

China's major festivals, when family, relatives and friends gather, are: Spring Festival, Lantern Festival, Qingming Festival, Dragon Boat Festival and Mid-autumn Festival. The custom of each festival is different. For example, at the Spring Festival the whole family get together to wrap dumplings; at the Dragon Boat Festival people hold dragon boat races and wrap *zongzi*; and at the Mid-Autumn Festival people eat mooncakes. These customs have become the symbols of various festivals and are important elements of traditional Chinese culture.

Shopping Spree on November 11

November 11 is now called the "festival of singles." On this day, China's shopping websites such as taobao, tmall, and 360buy launch discount shopping activities which trigger festival rushes. This phenomenon indicates that online shopping has become the new shopping trend for the Chinese people today.

Spring Festival

In the olden days, when the lunar calendar was in use, the first day of the first lunar month was the beginning of the new year. After the Revolution of 1911 China adopted the Gregorian calendar. To distinguish the lunar New Year's Day from

Jiaozi, symbolizing reunion and happiness

A foreign student performing the dragon dance during the Lantern Festival of 2014, Zhejiang Province

that of the Gregorian calendar, the former came to be called "Spring Festival," and generally falls between the last 10 days of January and mid-February. The Eve of the Spring Festival is an important time for family reunions, when many people stay up all night, "seeing the old year out." During the Spring Festival various traditional activities are enjoyed, including lion dances, dragon lantern dances, land boat rowing and stilt walking.

Lantern Festival

The Lantern Festival falls on the 15th day of the first lunar month, the first full moon night after the Spring Festival. Traditionally, people eat *yuanxiao*, and admire lanterns on the evening of this day. *Yuanxiao*, round balls of glutinous rice flour with sweet fillings, symbolize reunion. The tradition of viewing lanterns emerged in the first century AD, and is still popular across the country.

Qingming Festival

The Qingming Festival falls around April 5 every year. Traditionally, this is an occasion for people to make cer-

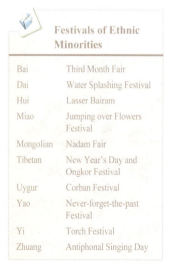

Festivals of Ethnic Minorities

Bai	Third Month Fair
Dai	Water Splashing Festival
Hui	Lasser Bairam
Miao	Jumping over Flowers Festival
Mongolian	Nadam Fair
Tibetan	New Year's Day and Ongkor Festival
Uygur	Corban Festival
Yao	Never-forget-the-past Festival
Yi	Torch Festival
Zhuang	Antiphonal Singing Day

Vast rape flower fields for sightseeing, April 6, 2014, Jiangsu Province

Zongzi, food for the Dragon Boat Festival

Holidays of the Gregorian Calendar

New Year's Day (January 1)
International Working Women's Day (March 8)
International Workers' Day (May 1)
Chinese Youth Day (May 4)
International Children's Day (June 1)
Army Day (August 1)
Teachers' Day (September 10)
National Day (November 1)

emonial offerings to their ancestors. It is also a time to pay respects to revolutionary martyrs. At this time of the year the weather begins to turn warm, and vegetation is bursting into new life. People like to go on outings, fly kites and enjoy the beauty of spring. That is why the festival is also called "Spring Outing Day."

Dragon Boat Festival

The Dragon Boat Festival falls on the fifth day of the fifth lunar month, when the weather is turning warm and insects awake from hibernation. This festival is said to honor the patriotic poet Qu Yuan (c. 340 BC-278 BC) of the State of Chu during the Warring States Period. Failing to realize his political ideals and hold back the decline of his state, Qu Yuan drowned himself in despair in the Miluo River on the fifth day of the fifth lunar month. Every year thereafter, on this day people go boating on rivers and throw bamboo tubes filled with rice into the water. Today, the memory of Qu Yuan lives on, as *zongzi* (glutinous rice wrapped pyramid-fashion in bamboo or reed leaves) are eaten and dragon boat races are held.

Mid-autumn Festival

The Mid-autumn Festival falls on the 15th day of the eighth lunar month, in the middle of autumn. In ancient times, people offered pastries or "mooncakes" to the Moon Goddess on this day. After the ceremony, the family would sit together to share the "mooncakes." The festival came to symbolize family reunions, as did the "mooncakes," and the custom has been passed down to this day.

Mooncake, food for the Mid-Autumn Festival

中 国 C h i n a

The People's Republic of China celebrated its 65th birthday in 2014. These 65 years of ups and downs witnessed the country's founding ceremony in 1949 and its rapid economic growth after launching the reform and opening up policies in the late 1970s. These important events, which formed turning points for this country, are all milestones for its development. Like footsteps, they record the road of China during the past 65 years.

65 Years of the People's Republic

- The Early Years of the People's Republic
- Exploration for Development
- The Ten Years of the "Cultural Revolution"
- Historical Shift
- The New Century

The Early Years of the People's Republic (1949-1956)

China experienced a rebirth in social systems, economic development and diplomatic conditions.

On October 1, 1949, Chairman Mao Zedong solemnly proclaimed on the Tiananmen Rostrum the establishment of the Central People's Government of the People's Republic of China.

In 1951, marked by the peaceful liberation of Tibet, China realized the unification of its major territories, with the exception of Taiwan, Hong Kong and Macao and a few other offshore islands.

1949   **1950**   **1951**

Panchen Erdeni called on the lamas of Ta'er Lamasery to donate to build fighter aircraft and cannons for the War to Resist US Aggression and Aid Korea.

In 1950, in response to the urgent call for military aid by the Democratic People's Republic of Korea (DPRK), the Chinese People's Volunteer Army marched to the front to fight side by side with the people of the DPRK, and achieved victory in the War to Resist US Aggression and Aid Korea.

The Agrarian Reform Law (June 30, 1950) announced the confiscation of lands of landlords and the division of them to peasants. Landlords had their shares too. Pictured is a laborer who had never had any livestock getting an ox as part of the agrarian reform.

In 1954 a diplomatic conference of China, the USSR, the US, the UK and France was held in Geneva, as the first significant international conference that China took part in as a big country after the founding of the PRC.

Chinese Premier Zhou Enlai entering the meeting place of the Geneva Conference.

● 1953　　　　● 1954　　　　● 1956

Dushanzi base of China-Soviet Union Oil Company

In 1953 China initiated the First Five-year Plan, with 156 modern industrial projects launched for overall national industrialization.

In 1956 China completed its socialist transformation of agriculture, handicrafts, and capitalist industry and commerce, marking the establishment of the socialist economic system in China.

Exploration for Development (1957-1965)

This was a period of historic exploration in the development of the People's Republic. As much needed to be done, all Chinese people were fired with enthusiasm for socialist construction.

A harvest of grain after the agricultural cooperatives movement started

In 1958 China launched the movement for establishing people's communes, by merging small agricultural cooperatives in rural areas so as to promote the commune governance system.

From 1959 to 1961 China suffered frequent natural disasters, which caused direct economic losses of 20 billion yuan.

1958 **1959** **1964**

In the same year, the "Great Leap Forward" was started, which resulted in great losses for the national economy.

An irrigation project

The mushroom cloud from China's first atom bomb test

In 1964 China's successfully tested its first atom bomb. That same day, the Chinese government solemnly proclaimed that China would never take the initiative in using nuclear weapons at any time or under any circumstances. Three years later, China successfully tested its first hydrogen bomb.

The Ten Years of the "Cultural Revolution" (1966-1976)

The 10 years of the "cultural revolution" was a time of turmoil, which pushed the People's Republic to the edge of economic breakdown.

In February 1972 US President Nixon visited China, symbolizing the normalization of Sino-US relations. The two countries issued the Shanghai Communiqué reiterating the "One China" principle. That same year, Sino-Japanese relations were also normalized.

In May 1966 the "cultural revolution" was launched.

In 1974 Mao Zedong proposed the "Three Worlds" theory when meeting with Kenneth Kaunda, president of Zambia.

● 1966 ● 1970 ● 1971 ● 1972 ● 1974 ● 1976

People watching the launching of the DFH satellite

In 1970 the first man-made earth satellite designed and manufactured by China, the DFH-1, was successfully launched.

In 1971 a US ping-pong team visited China for an invitational tournament; and "ping-pong diplomacy" opened the door to establishing Sino-US relations. On October 25, the 26th Session of the UN General Assembly (UNGA) proclaimed the restoration of all the lawful rights of the PRC in the United Nations.

In 1976 Zhou Enlai, Zhu De and Mao Zedong, three of the major founders of the PRC, passed away in succession. The same year, the 10 years of the "cultural revolution" ended with the smashing of the "Gang of Four."

Qiao Guanhua (L) and Huang Hua headed the Chinese delegation to the 26th Session of the UNGA.

Historical Shift (1977-1999)

The year 1978 was a significant shifting point in China's history, when the reform and opening up policy was launched. By adopting this mode of development, China has rapidly grown into a new period of advance.

Peking University awaited its first batch of new students in spring of 1978 after the university entrance exam system was restored.

In 1977 the university entrance exam system was restored. University enrolment followed the principle of unified examination and competitive merit.

● 1977　　● 1978　　● 1979　　● 1980

Today's Shenzhen

In 1978 in Beijing, the Third Plenary Session of the 11th CPC Central Committee was held, which proposed the transfer of the work focus toward modernization construction.

From 1980 special economic zones were officially set up in Shenzhen, Zhuhai, Shantou, Xiamen and Hainan.

On January 1, 1979 the Standing Committee of the NPC issued the Message to Compatriots in Taiwan, proposing respect for Taiwan's current situation, and "Three Direct Links" (mail, transport and trade) across the Taiwan Straits. On the same day, Sino-US diplomatic relations were officially established.

The socialist market economy picked up speed. A farmers' market

In 1982 Deng Xiaoping proposed building socialism with Chinese characteristics, as part of Deng Xiaoping Theory. The same year, China deepened rural economic structural reform and promoted the household contract responsibility system with remuneration linked to output.

Deng Xiaoping inspected Shenzhen on January 22, 1992

In 1992 Deng Xiaoping made an inspection tour of Wuchang, Shenzhen, Zhuhai and Shanghai, and delivered significant speeches to trigger a new upsurge in reform and opening up.

● 1982　　● 1986　　● 1992　　● 1993

Chinese women's volleyball players won their first championship on November 16, 1981.

By 1986 the Chinese women's volleyball team had won five successive championships, which was unprecedented in the world and became the symbol of China's growing national power.

In April 1993 the Wang-Koo Talks were held in Singapore, marking the first meeting between the top leaders of the non-government institutions of Taiwan and the mainland dealing with cross-Straits affairs, as well as the first communication between senior figures from both sides of the Taiwan Straits in more than 40 years.

CHINA

In 1995 the reincarnated "soul boy" of the 10th Panchen Erdeni was confirmed through the traditional lot-drawing from a gold urn. The State Council approved Gyaltsen Norbu as the 11th Panchen Erdeni.

On October 1, 1999 a military parade and celebration for the 50th anniversary of the founding of the PRC was held in Beijing.

1995 1997 1998 1999

On July 1, 1997 the Chinese government resumed its exercise of sovereignty over Hong Kong, putting into practice the "one country, two systems" principle.

On December 20, 1999 Macao returned to the motherland.

In 1998 China succeeded in surviving the one-year Asian Financial Crisis. During the crisis, as a responsible country, China agreed not to devalue the RMB, which avoided a new round of currency devaluation in crisis-stricken countries.

The New Century (2000-2014)

The new century has witnessed rapid development for China in all fields. Further merging with the rest of the world, China has followed the right direction to advance with full confidence.

On February 25, 2000 Jiang Zemin first gave a detailed explanation of the Three Represents* during an inspection tour of Guangdong Province.

* The Three Represents designates that the CPC represents the development trends of the advanced productive forces, the orientation of advanced culture and the fundamental interests of the overwhelming majority of the people of China.

In June 2001 the Shanghai Cooperation Organization was established.

On October 21, 2001, the Ninth APEC Economic Leaders' Meetings was held in Shanghai. Following that, the Beijing Summit of the Forum on China-Africa Cooperation, the Asia-Europe Meeting and the Six-Party Talks were held in China.

● 2000   ● 2001

On June 26, 2000 the working draft of the human genome project was successfully completed, with the participation of China as the sole developing country.

Representatives to the 4th WTO Ministerial Conference applauding China's entry to the organization.

On November 10, 2001 China entered the World Trade Organization (WTO).

In 2003 China achieved a victory over the SARS epidemic.

On October 15, 2003, China successfully launched its first manned spacecraft, *Shenzhou-5*, which fulfilled the nation's millenary space aviation dream.

On January 1, 2006 the Regulations on Agricultural Taxes was abolished, and the history of over 2,000 years of agricultural taxes officially came to an end.

On April 29, 2005 talks between Hu Jintao, General Secretary of the CPC Central Committee, and Kuomintang Chairman Lien Chan were held in Beijing, as the first official talks between the supreme leaders of the two parties in 60 years.

Farmers were overjoyed at the abolition of agricultural taxes.

● 2003   ● 2005   ● 2006   ● 2007

On July 1, 2006 the Qinghai-Tibet Railway, the longest plateau railway with the highest elevation and with the longest distance traveling through permafrost, was opened to traffic.

In 2007 the 17th National Congress of the CPC was held, at which the Scientific Outlook on Development was put forward.

On May 12, 2008 an earthquake measuring 8.0 on the Richter scale struck Wenchuan, in Sichuan Province. The most devastating earthquake China had encountered since its founding in 1949 caused huge losses. Under the guidance of the CPC and the government, the united Chinese people triumphed over the disaster.

On May 12, 2009 the 83rd plenary meeting of the 63rd Session of the UN General Assembly convened at the UN Headquarters in New York to reelect its 18 members of the Human Rights Council. Representatives from 191 UN members attended and voted. With 167 votes, China was reappointed as a member of the Human Rights Council for a term of four years – from 2009 to 2012.

2008　　　　2009

In 2008, facing the severe situation of the global financial crisis, China practiced flexible and prudent macro-economic policies to maintain steady economic growth.

In September 2008 the *Shenzhou-7* manned spacecraft was successfully launched, realizing China's first spacewalk.

In November 2008 ARATS Chairman Chen Yunlin visited Taiwan, marking an ARATS leader's first official trip to Taiwan. Abiding by a signed agreement, the "Three Direct Links" across the Taiwan Straits were basically realized on December 15.

In August and September 2008 Beijing successfully hosted the Olympics followed by the Paralympic Games. China fulfilled its promise of "Two Games of Equal Splendor," and was highly praised worldwide.

On April 30, 2010 the opening ceremony of the 41st World Expo was held at the Expo Center in Shanghai. On May 1 the Shanghai World Expo formally opened to the public. Attracting 246 countries and international organizations, it was the largest-ever expo, with the theme of "Better City, Better Life."

On September 25, 2012 China's first aircraft carrier, the *Liaoning* was commissioned into the Navy of the Chinese People's Liberation Army after sea trials. Approved by the Central Military Commission, the *Liaoning* got its present name, and received the side designation "16."

● 2010   ● 2011   ● 2012

On July 1, 2011 a grand gathering marking the 90th anniversary of the CPC was held in the Great Hall of the People in Beijing.

On October 11, 2012 the Swedish Academy announced that the 2012 Nobel Prize for Literature had been awarded to Chinese writer Mo Yan, who was the first Chinese to win this prize.

From November 8 to 14, 2012 the 18th National Congress of the CPC was held in Beijing.

From November 9 to 12, 2013, the Third Plenary Session of the 18th Central Committee of the CPC was held in Beijing, at which the Decision of the Central Committee of the Communist Party of China on Some Major Issues Concerning Comprehensively Deepening the Reform was adopted.

The Fourth CICA Summit was held at Shanghai Expo Center on May 20-21, with the theme "On Enhancing Dialogue, Trust and Coordination for a New Asia of Peace, Stability and Cooperation." It was presided over by Chinese President Xi Jinping. China assumed CICA Chairmanship for the period 2014-16.

2013　　　2014

On December 2, 2013 China launched the *Chang'e-3* lunar probe from the Xichang Satellite Launch Center in Sichuan Province.

On December 14, *Chang'e-3* landed on the near side of the moon, to the east of Sinus Iridum (Bay of Rainbows).

On December 15, China's first lunar rover *Yutu*, carried by *Chang'e-3*, was successfully deployed from the lander, enabling the Five-Starred Red Flag to make its debut on the moon.

Appendix

Government Websites

- Chinese Government
  http://www.gov.cn
- Information Office of the State Council
  http://www.scio.gov.cn
- Ministry of Foreign Affairs
  http://www.fmprc.gov.cn/
- Ministry of National Defense
  http://www.mod.gov.cn/
- National Development and Reform Commission
  http://www.ndrc.gov.cn/
- Ministry of Education
  http://www.moe.gov.cn/
- Ministry of Science and Technology
  http://www.most.gov.cn/
- Ministry of Industry and Information Technology
  http://www.miit.gov.cn/
- State Ethnic Affairs Commission
  http://www.seac.gov.cn/
- Ministry of Public Security
  http://www.mps.gov.cn/
- Ministry of Supervision
  http://www.ccdi.gov.cn/
- Ministry of Civil Affairs
  http://www.mca.gov.cn/
- Ministry of Justice
  http://www.moj.gov.cn/
- Ministry of Finance
  http://www.mof.gov.cn/
- Ministry of Human Resources and Social Security
  http://www.mohrss.gov.cn/
- Ministry of Land and Resources
  http://www.mlr.gov.cn/
- Ministry of Environmental Protection
  http://www.zhb.gov.cn/
- Ministry of Housing and Urban-Rural Development
  http://www.mohurd.gov.cn/
- Ministry of Transport
  http://www.moc.gov.cn/
- Ministry of Water Resources
  http://www.mwr.gov.cn/
- Ministry of Agriculture
  http://www.moa.gov.cn/
- Ministry of Commerce
  http://www.mofcom.gov.cn/
- Ministry of Culture
  http://www.ccnt.gov.cn/
- National Health and Family Planning Commission
  http://www.nhfpc.gov.cn/
- People's Bank of China
  http://www.pbc.gov.cn/
- National Audit Office
  http://www.audit.gov.cn/

China on the Internet

- News Agencies
  Xinhua News Agency
  http://www.news.cn
  China News Agency
  http://www.chinanews.com

Appendix 237

- TV
  CCTV
  http://www.cctv.com

- Radio
  China Radio International
  http://www.cri.cn

- External Publicity
  China International Publishing Group
  http://www.cipg.org.cn
  China International Communication Center
  http://www.cicc.org.cn

- Website
  China Internet Information Center
  http://www.china.com.cn

- Newspapers
  People's Daily
  http://www.people.com.cn
  China Daily
  http://chinadaily.com.cn

- Magazines
  Beijing Review
  http://www.bjreview.com.cn
  China Today
  http://www.chinatoday.com.cn
  China Pictorial
  http://www.rmhb.com.cn
  People's China
  http://www.peoplechina.com.cn
  Women of China
  http://www.womenofchina.com

- Books
  Foreign Languages Press
  http://www.flp.com.cn
  New World Press
  http://www.nwp.com.cn
  Sinolingua
  http://www.sinolingua.com.cn
  Blossom Press
  http://www.blossompress.com.cn
  Dolphin Books
  http://www.dolphin-books.com.cn
  China Pictorial Publishing House
  http://www.zghbcbs.com
  New Star Press
  http://www.newstarpress.com

- International Publications Distribution
  China International Book Trading Corporation
  http://www.cibtc.com.cn

- Travel Agencies
  China International Travel Service Head Office
  http://www.cits.com.cn/
  China Travel Service Head Office
  http://www.ctsho.com
  China Youth Travel Service Tours Holding Co., Ltd
  http://www.cytsonline.com
  China Comfort Travel Co., Ltd
  http://www.cct.cn
  CITIC Travel Co., Ltd
  http://www.travel.citic.com

图书在版编目(CIP)数据

中国.2014：英文/钟欣编；外文出版社英文部译.—北京：外文出版社，2014
ISBN 978-7-119-08945-4

Ⅰ.①中… Ⅱ.①钟…②外… Ⅲ.①社会主义建设成就－中国－2014－英文 Ⅳ.①D619

中国版本图书馆CIP数据核字(2014)第169084号

出版指导：	徐 步 解 琛
中文审定：	萧师铃
责任编辑：	文 芳 蔡莉莉 王际洲 陈丝纶
撰 稿：	崔黎丽 王传民 潘 灯 周 彪 王奎庭 王振红 陆 宁 钟 平 等
英文翻译：	冯 鑫 严 晶 曲 磊 王 玮 徐汀汀
英文改稿：	Paul White
英文审定：	韩清月
图片来源：	新华社 中国新闻社 中国国家博物馆 人民画报社 视觉中国 东方IC 全景视觉 汉华易美
	陈 胜 陈顺国 陈卫东 陈显耀 邓 佳 董 宁 杜泽泉 方东风 郭晓勇 胡兆明 黄 辉 黄君毅 晋守贤 兰建琼 李 涓 李晓钢 李晓英 李有祥 刘世昭 楼庆西 茹遂初 沈 影 孙树明 唐少文 屠国啸 王汝春 吴晓军 徐腾长 银道禄 虞向军 张书奇 周剑生 等（以姓氏音序为序）
数据来源：	国家统计局 国务院新闻办公室 新华社 中国网 中国发展门户网 等
装帧设计：	北京大盟文化艺术有限公司 北京维诺传媒文化有限公司
审 图 号：	GS（2014）2006号
印刷监制：	冯 浩

（本书个别图片未能联系上作者，敬请与出版社联系，将及时支付稿酬。感谢！）

中国 2014

钟 欣 编

出 版 人：	徐 步
出版发行：	外文出版社有限责任公司
地　　址：	北京市西城区百万庄大街24号　　邮政编码：100037
网　　址：	http://www.flp.com.cn　　电子邮箱：flp@cipg.org.cn
电　　话：	008610-68320579（总编室）　008610-68996158（编辑部）
	008610-68995852（发行部）　008610-68996183（投稿电话）
印　　刷：	鸿博昊天科技有限公司
经　　销：	新华书店／外文书店
开　　本：	787mm×1092mm　1/16　　印张：15.5　　字数：200千
版　　次：	2014年12月第1版第1次印刷
书　　号：	ISBN 978-7-119-08945-4
定　　价：	129.00元

版权所有　侵权必究　如有印装问题本社负责调换（电话：68329904）